THE FUNDING LOTTERY

Student financial support in further education and its impact on participation

Alicia Herbert and Claire Callender

POLICY STUDIES INSTITUTE
London

The publishing imprint of the independent
POLICY STUDIES INSTITUTE
100 Park Village East, London NW1 3SR
Tel. 0171 468 0468   Fax. 0171 388 0914

ISBN 0 85374 740 7

Cover design by Russell Stretten Consultancy
Laserset by Policy Studies Institute
Printed in Great Britain by Oakdale Printing Company Ltd, Bournemouth

THE FUNDING LOTTERY

Policy Studies Institute (PSI) is one of Europe's leading independent research organisations undertaking studies of economic, industrial and social policy and the workings of political institutions.

PSI is a registered charity, run on a non-profit basis, and is not associated with any political party, pressure group or commercial interest.

PSI attaches great importance to covering a wide range of subject areas with its multi-disciplinary approach. The Institute's researchers are organised in groups which currently cover the following programmes:

Crime, Justice and Youth Studies – Employment – Ethnic Equality and Diversity – Family Finances – Information and Citizenship – Information and Cultural Studies – Social Care and Health Studies – Work, Benefits and Social Participation

This publication arises from the Family Finances group and is one of over 30 publications made available by the Institute each year.

Information about the work of PSI and a catalogue of publications can be obtained from

Publications Department, Policy Studies Institute,
100 Park Village East, London NW1 3SR

Other relevant PSI publications include:

Payne, J and Callender, C (1997) *Student Loans: Who borrows and why?* London: PSI

Callender, C and Kempson, E (1996) *Student Finances: Income, expenditure and take-up of student loans.* London: PSI

CONTENTS

Acknowledgements   vii

Executive summary   ix

1   Introduction   1

    1.1   Introduction   1

    1.2   Background to the research   1

    1.3   Research aims   2

    1.4   Remit of the study   2

    1.5   Methodology   3

    1.6   Structure of the report   3

2   The costs of further education and funding sources   4

    2.1   Introduction   4

    2.2   What are the costs of further education and training?   4

    2.3   What are the key funding sources?   6

    2.4   What are the trends and developments in funding for learners?   20

    2.5   Summary   22

3   Researching the role of financial support   23

    3.1   Introduction   23

    3.2   Why is there a lack of research in Britain on participation and financial support, compared to the United States?   23

    3.3   What is the nature of the research on participation and financial support?   25

    3.4   What are the limitations of British research on participation and financial support?   25

    3.5   Summary   28

4   Financial support and access   29

   4.1   Introduction   29

   4.2   What are the participation and non-participation levels?   29

   4.3   What non-financial factors affect access to further education and training?   31

   4.4   Does financial support act as an incentive?   33

   4.5   Does the lack of financial support act as a disincentive?   36

   4.6   How does the lack of financial support affect particular groups of students?   39

   4.7   Summary   43

5   Financial support, retention and achievement   44

   5.1   Introduction   44

   5.2   What are the non-completion levels?   44

   5.3   What non-financial factors affect completion and achievement?   47

   5.4   Does financial support act as an incentive?   51

   5.5   Does the lack of financial support act as a disincentive?   52

   5.6   How does the lack of financial support affect particular groups of students?   55

   5.7   Conclusion   56

6   Learning accounts   57

   6.1   Introduction   57

   6.2   What are the origins of the learning accounts?   57

   6.3   What are the different models of learning accounts?   58

   6.4   Summary   62

References   63

Acknowledgements

We owe our thanks to many people, in particular to Helena Kennedy QC who showed a deep commitment and interest in our work. Our thanks also go to the members of the FEFC's Widening Participation Committee for their support, and especially to Emily Thrane, the Committee's secretary. At PSI we would like to thank Sue Johnson, our librarian, Siân Putnam and Karin Erskine for helping to produce a handsome looking report.

Executive summary

INTRODUCTION

In 1994 the Further Education Funding Council (FEFC) established the Widening Participation Committee, chaired by Helena Kennedy QC, to advise on ways in which it can encourage more people to participate, succeed and progress in further education.[1]

The Policy Studies Institute was commissioned by the Council to undertake a review of existing literature and research on student financial support in the further education sector and its impact on participation. This report outlines the findings of that study.

Research aims

The overall aim of the research was to identify and summarise published literature and recent research relating to the contribution made by financial support for learners to their participation in further education and training. In particular, it sought to identify the role of financial support in:

- motivating initial access to education and training
- inhibiting or enabling access, success and progression
- rewarding or providing an incentive for success and progression.

In addition, the study reports on current ideas about individual learning accounts and their impact on participation.

METHODOLOGY

The research consisted exclusively of desk research. It involved:

- a variety of library searches at institutions such as the FEFC, Department for Education and Employment, London School of Economics, and Institute of Education
- explorations of a wide range of databases both in Britain and the United States such as ERIC, PsychLit, EconLit, and SocioLit

---

1   For the full report of the Committee's recommendations see Kennedy, H. (1997) *Learning Works: Widening Participation in Further Education.* Coventry: Further Education Funding Council.

- some informal telephone interviews with representatives from a range of key organisations such as the Association of Colleges, charities, Institute of Education, DfEE, Inland Revenue, and the Unemployment Unit.

RESEARCH FINDINGS

The costs of further education (Chapter 2)

No research exists which has sought to systematically quantify the costs of participating in further education for different types of learners. However, it is now recognised that the key direct and indirect costs include:

- course fees
- add-on costs associated with learning such as books, examination fees
- direct personal and family support costs
- opportunity costs
- childcare and dependent relative care costs
- transport costs
- technical support aids needed by students with special needs.

Sources of funding (Chapter 2)

There is no comprehensive or universal system of financial support for individuals in further education, unlike provisions for full-time students in higher education. Students in FE are the 'poor relation' of these HE students in terms of access to funding, and the type and level of financial support available. This is despite the fact that their financial need is likely to be greater, given their socio-economic characteristics.

Access to financial support for FE students is a lottery. The funds are not distributed in accordance with notions of equity or need. The receipt of funds is often discretionary, dictated by the decisions and policies of a range of gatekeepers. Students in financial need, facing similar circumstances, are treated very differently depending on their age, where they live or what they study. Rarely can the financial support be guaranteed or relied upon. Moreover, on the whole, this funding situation has deteriorated in recent years. This has resulted in yet a further shift in the burden of financial responsibility for FE on to the individual learner.

Individuals can receive financial support from the following key sources:

- *Discretionary awards* made by Local Education Authorities directly to individuals under Section 2 of the 1962 Education Act. These awards are the main source of public funds for non-HE students in post-compulsory education, aimed explicitly at meeting the costs of participation. Yet some local authorities no longer award them and only a very small minority of all FE students receive them.

  Of the 3 million students enrolled at colleges in the further education sector in England in 1994/95 only about 162,000 received discretionary awards – representing about one in 20 or 5 per cent of all FE students in England. By contrast, about three-quarters of all full-time students in higher education in the UK received a mandatory grant from their local authority and about three out of five received government subsidies through the receipt of student loans, irrespective of their financial need (Payne and Callender, 1997).

Since 1992/93 expenditure on discretionary awards has fallen by a third. The number of people receiving awards peaked in 1993/94 but has since fallen to pre-1991/92 levels. Particularly marked has been the steep drop in the number of adults receiving awards. As a result of these trends, the overall value of awards has fallen by 30 per cent since 1990/91.

In 1994/95 the average value of an award was £665, for the minority who received them. This sum is not sufficient to meet the full costs of participation. By contrast, in 1995/96 the average value of a mandatory maintenance grant (excluding fees) for all full-time undergraduate HE students in the UK was £1,726 and £1,327 for those students living at home. In addition, they could top up this grant with a student loan – the average value of which was £1,243 (Callender and Kempson, 1996).

However, the discretionary nature of these awards for FE students means that the amount an individual receives, and what it covers, varies enormously from one local authority to another. Much more important, some students do not receive an award at all, despite their financial need. They have to rely on their families for support, yet their families may be in no position to offer such support.

The system of discretionary awards has become a lottery. The receipt of awards is dependent on where the students live or what they study, rather than on their financial need or even academic merit. There are no guarantees that a student will receive any funds from this source.

- *Access funds* were introduced by the government in 1990/91 for students aged 19 and over where financial hardship may inhibit access to FE and HE.

FE is allocated about 20 per cent of the total government budget on Access funds while the remainder goes to HE. This is despite the fact that a much higher proportion of students in FE than HE come from low social economic groups and thus a higher proportion have a need for financial help.

In 1995/96, 46,878 students in the FE sector in England received Access funds – about 1.5 per cent of all students in the sector. They received on average £95 (FEFC unpublished data). By contrast, in 1995/96, 5 per cent of full-time undergraduates in the UK gained money from Access funds, and the average amount they received was three times greater – £358[2] (Callender and Kempson, 1996).

Access funds, like Local Education Authority awards, are a lottery. They too are highly discretionary. It is up to individual colleges to decide how, and to whom, to disburse these funds among the eligible applicants. Like discretionary awards, they are an unreliable source of funding. There are no guarantees that a student will receive such financial support. As important, the level of support received by students on average is very low, it does not meet the full costs of participation, and the amount they receive has fallen in recent years.

- *Fee remission* is a very important indirect form of financial support. All young people in further education under the age of 19 years do not have to pay tuition fees. In addition, certain groups of adults on low incomes, those receiving means-tested social security benefits and those following certain courses, have their fees remitted. Following the introduction of the 1992 Education Act other groups are also eligible. Since incorporation, remission policies have been set nationally by the FEFC rather than by

---

2   This figure includes money received from both their institutions' Access and Hardship fund.

individual LEAs. Thus a significant source of unequal treatment has been eradicated but the policy remains selective.

In 1995/96, 1.3 million individuals in England had their fees remitted – representing about a third of all students in the FE sector. The majority (71 per cent) of these had their fees waivered rather than being exempt under the 1992 Act. The policy, however, leaves untouched the issue of certain add-on costs and student maintenance. In addition, it excludes certain groups of low income students such as those on non-means tested social security benefits.

Although remission policies in FE have improved, it should be noted that fees in higher education are treated very differently. Currently, the vast majority of full-time home undergraduate students do not pay any fees. Nor is the payment of fees in HE related to either a student's age or income.[3]

- *Government training programmes* aimed primarily at the unemployed offer some financial support for its participants.

In 1995/96, 251,000 young people started a Youth Training (YT) programme in England and 25,900 started in the government's Modern Apprenticeship programme. They have their main training costs covered via their local TEC, including add-on costs. Some also receive their transport costs. In addition, they receive a training allowance, or a wage.

YT allowances currently stand at £30 a week for 16 year olds and £35 for 17 to 18 year olds. Although participants are guaranteed funding, the allowances had been frozen until April 1997 when they were increased by 50p. They have not kept pace with inflation which brings into question their effectiveness as incentives for people to enter training. Moreover, there is an element of lottery in terms of the money trainees receive. Some employers and training providers are paying higher than the minimum training allowance but about a third of trainees only get the basic allowance.

Training for Work (TfW) is the main route open to the adult unemployed wishing to gain a qualification. It too covers the key course costs. Participants get their social security benefits plus a £10 weekly top-up. Any travel expenses or living away from home allowance does not affect the amount of benefit they receive. This top-up has remained the same since 1986 and does not cover all the add-on costs associated with training.

- *Social security benefits* are another essential source of financial support for at least 100,000 unemployed individuals in the FE sector. However, since the introduction of the Job Seekers' Allowance in October 1996, individuals can claim benefits only if they study for less than 16 guided learning hours a week, and remain 'available for' and 'actively seek' full-time work. If they fail to meet these conditions, they can have their entitlement to social security benefits withdrawn.

There is nothing secure about this source of funding. Students may have to stop studying to protect their benefit entitlement. The rules act as a major disincentive to study among a particularly vulnerable group who are especially likely to benefit from access to education and training.

Yet again, like other sources of funding, there is an element of a lottery at play. The extent to which colleges can be flexible in their provision, to allow claimants to continue with courses if they get a job, varies depending on the college and the course. Perhaps

---

3   This is likely to change following the Dearing Report and other government proposals.

more important, the rules are so complicated and confusing that, in practice, they may not be operated consistently either by Employment Service offices or by colleges across the country.

- *The European Social Fund* pays for the unemployed and socially disadvantaged groups to participate in education and training. However, not all colleges apply for or succeed in accessing these funds. They have to compete for funds with TECs, higher education, and the voluntary sector.

  1996 ESF Allocations (Objective 3) to the FE sector were £70 million which represented about 16 per cent of the total allocations. So overall, the FE sector gets only a small proportion of the overall ESF budget.

  In 1995 approximately £42 million were allocated to the FE sector in England, covering about 120,000 beneficiaries. The funding is matched by colleges and most was used to cover the direct and add-on cost of training. Some colleges, however, also use the funds to pay for benefits in kind, such as childcare provision. Once again, access to these type of payments in kind varies from college to college. And unlike training sponsored by the ESF in the voluntary sector, few colleges provide training allowances, free transport or other payments in kind, such as meal vouchers.

- *Career Development Loans* for individuals to pay for employment-related courses were introduced in 1988. Overall take-up has been lower than originally anticipated primarily because individuals are concerned about getting into debt. According to the CDLs Annual Report, in 1995/96 some 13,000 loans were awarded, a drop of 12 per cent on the previous year. The initiative has had little impact on the FE sector. Nor is it promoting a wide range of vocational training as originally planned, rather it has become a vehicle for graduates to finance post-graduate courses.

- *Tax relief* on vocational training was introduced in 1992 for individuals not in receipt of any financial assistance, and other tax concessions were introduced in the 1997 budget. Such concessions mean, for instance, that tuition fees are reduced, but they help only a minority and are of use primarily to employed people with access to funding or credit. Those most in need of education and training are unlikely to be in well-paid jobs or to be able to pay for their fees, and so benefit from this concession.

- *Employers* are the final main source of financial support for those participating in further education. Accurate data on the numbers gaining such support in the sector and the exact type of financial support they receive, are not readily available. Figures do show that the number of employer-led part-time enrolments in FE colleges fell by 16 per cent between 1988 and 1993 to 305,000 and the fall was much greater for 16–18 year olds.

  It is well established that not all employees have equal access to employer-sponsored education and training. Those most disadvantaged in the labour market have the least access. So once again there is an element of a lottery, but the odds favour employees in well-paid jobs higher up the occupational ladder.

  The current system of financial support in FE is full of anomlies and it is neither fair nor transparent. The system favours young, full-time, academic learners while penalising adults, part-time and vocationally oriented/focused learners.

The absence of research on the impact of financial support on participation (Chapter 3)

Unlike the United States, there is no history in Britain of conducting research on the relationship between participation and student support in further or higher education. Consequently, there is a dearth of such studies in Britain. Key British studies which have examined the issues of initial access to FE, drop-out and progression have mostly failed to explore the impact of financial support on these issues. These studies have tended to be preoccupied with the impact of social class rather than either income or financial aid.

The gaps in research are particularly pronounced in relation to studies on the costs of participation and on the role of student support on initial access, and especially progression.

The few studies which has been conducted are limited both in their scale and in the methods used. As a result, it is very difficult to generalise from these studies or to give an accurate assessment of the impact of financial support on participation.

Financial support and access to further education (Chapter 4)

There is a limited amount of research in Britain which shows that financial support acts as an incentive to initial access to further education. In particular, training allowances and fee remission policies have been shown to have a positive effect. Conversely, the lack of such financial support is often cited as a disincentive especially for adults, unemployed people and women. Financial barriers to participation include tuition fees, the add-on costs of training and other indirect costs such as childcare.

Various national studies conducted in the United States have examined the enrolment behaviour of school leavers – high school students. These studies are primarily concerned with access to higher education including community colleges – which are the nearest equivalent that the American education system has to FE colleges in Britain. The studies show unequivocally that financial aid has a positive impact on student enrolment, especially among students from low-income families.

Research in the United States has been concerned to examine the impact on enrolments of changes both in tuition fees and the American equivalent to maintenance grants. Once again, there is a broad consensus in the research that increases in tuition costs depress enrolment levels among students from low-income groups but not those from high-income groups. Similarly, research shows that financial aid packages which include monies for maintenance also have a positive impact on enrolment, as do their value. Grants were found to be a more effective recruitment tool than loans, especially for the lowest income groups.

Financial support and drop-out (Chapter 5)

Research on the inter-relationship between drop-out and financial support has been conducted in Britain and the issue has become increasingly important with changes in the funding and inspection frameworks of colleges. There are, however, severe limitations to these studies. In particular, explanations for drop-out often are not based on students' own assessments and the circumstances of students dropping out are not compared with those who do not.

The conclusion of these studies is that there is no single cause of drop-out. Diverse factors affect various groups of students differently, in disparate organisational contexts. More significant, financial hardship is just one of many complex factors contributing to drop-out. When experienced in conjunction with course-related factors such as dissatisfaction with the quality of teaching and learning support, drop-out is more likely to occur.

Sociological studies in the United States have reached fairly similar, but more robust, conclusions. Most see attrition as attributed to a lack of congruency between students and their institutions. Financial aid has a significant total effect on persistence but only indirectly, by facilitating the 'fit' between students and their institutions.

Other types of research in the United States has modelled the interplay between persistence and financial support. It too shows a positive association between financial assistance and retention rates, especially when models separate out the effects of tuition costs and various forms of financial aid. However, students respond differently to cost issues when considering their initial enrolment and when making decisions about dropping out. Insufficient funds do lead to non-completion or to breaks in study, especially when tuition fees are high. In contrast, the availability of financial support has been shown to reduce the probability of low-income students dropping out.

There are no studies in Britain that have systematically examined the role of financial support on progression. Limited data on the destinations of FE college students are now more readily available. From this, information on progression can be extrapolated but such work has yet to be undertaken. Nor has this been a major focus of research in the United States. Research on enrolment reported above has examined the transfer of students from community colleges to four-year college programmes. It shows the importance of financial aid in encouraging such transfers.

Individual learning accounts (Chapter 6)

Various interesting models of learning accounts or learning banks have been proposed by a range of organisations and individuals aimed at promoting 'lifelong learning'. Most suggest that the state, employers and individuals should contribute to this account. It would be left to individuals to decide how to spend the monies in their account.

The precise focus, design, and operation of learning accounts is still to be defined. This makes it very difficult to assess their potential impact on increasing participation. However, any model which relies on contributions from employers or employees is likely to disadvantage the very groups most in need of further education and training – the unemployed, the self-employed and low-paid part-time workers.

The idea of learning accounts is an exciting one and could potentially overcome many of the problems associated with the current financial support system. However, many questions are yet to be addressed especially the issue of, and concerns about, debt.

CONCLUSION

Given the evidence from the American literature, it is beyond question that financial aid can widen participation in education, especially among low-income groups. However, the current funding system in Britain for further education students is totally inadequate and unfair. In its present form, it is likely to have only a minimal impact on widening participation. What is required is a comprehensive system of financial support which operates nationally, is transparent and flexible – balancing the needs of, and the costs incurred by, different types of students and learners.

Any such reforms would have to take into account the full range of funding policies and methodologies, and not those exclusively associated with student financial support.

To help inform such a review and policy developments, more research is required. First, research which accurately assesses the costs of participation is essential. Second, more systematic and robust research is required which is explicitly designed to assess the impact of financial support on initial access, completion and progression in FE. Such studies should include both participants and non-participants, completers and non-completers, and those who do and do not progress. They would need to assess the effectiveness of different types of student financial support and model the impact of differing amounts of financial aid on participation.

To aid such research, more data need to be collected, especially longitudinal data and data on potential entrants. In addition, current national data on participants in FE, although much improved of late, need to be made more comprehensive and accessible.

Chapter 1

Introduction

1.1 INTRODUCTION

In 1994 the Further Education Funding Council (FEFC) established the Widening Participation Committee, chaired by Helena Kennedy QC, to advise on ways in which it can encourage more people to participate, succeed and progress in further education.[4]

The Policy Studies Institute was commissioned by the Council to undertake a review of existing literature and research on student financial support in the further education sector and its impact on participation. This report outlines the findings of that study.

1.2 BACKGROUND TO THE RESEARCH

In 1995/96, some three and a half million students were enrolled at colleges in the further education sector in England alone. Nearly three-quarters of these were enrolled on provision funded by the FEFC. Enrolment and participation levels for both under 19 year olds and adults have grown dramatically over the past ten years but now appear to be slowing down.

The participation patterns for different age groups vary considerably, however. For example, three-quarters of students on FEFC funded provision are adults and the remainder are under 19. 'Traditional' 16–18 year olds now constitute less than a quarter of the students in Council funded provision and this trend is set to continue. Moreover, while the majority of adult students (90 per cent) are studying part-time, most under 19 year old students are full-time (72 per cent).[5]

The further education sector, therefore, appears now to be more accessible than ever before. Uden (1994) points out that, although these trends are encouraging, recent surveys show that the increased numbers of adult learners entering the sector do not seem to have made any significant impact on the *overall* composition of the adult learner population, which remains largely unrepresentative. It is still the case that learners are more likely to be middle-class and employed (Uden, 1994). Government statistics indicate that people from unskilled manual working backgrounds remain markedly under-represented in further education (Uden, 1994). It could, therefore, be said that participation in the sector has increased but not necessarily widened.

---

4 For the full report of the Committee's recommendations see Kennedy, H. (1997) *Learning Works: Widening Participation in Further Education.* Coventry: Further Education Funding Council.

5 Student numbers at colleges in the further education sector and external institutions in England, 1995–96, Press Release, FEFC, December 1996.

There are various ways to widen participation in the sector. One approach is to identify the barriers which are 'shared' by the under-represented groups and concentrate on removing them. Financial support or, the lack of it, is one such barrier: this is the focus of this report.

It is against this background that the Policy Studies Institute was commissioned to undertake this study.

1.3 RESEARCH AIMS

The overall aim of the research project was to identify and summarise published and recent research relating to the contribution made by financial support for learners to their participation in further education and training. In particular, it was originally intended to identify the role of financial support in:

- motivating initial access to education and training;
- inhibiting or enabling access, success and progression;
- rewarding or providing incentives for success and progression.

In addition, the study was to report on current ideas about individual learning accounts.

As the research progressed the research aims described above had to be modified. In particular, it was not possible to investigate in any detail the impact of financial support on progression because of the lack of research conducted in this area. There are no studies in Britain that have systematically examined the role of financial support on progression. Limited data on the destinations of further education college students are now available from which information on progression could be extrapolated but this was outside the remit of this study. However, the lack of research is, in itself, an important finding.

1.4 REMIT OF THE STUDY

1.4.1 Defining 'student'

In this report, the generic term 'student' has been adopted although we recognise that some people may be employees. No distinction is made between the terms 'student' and 'learner', they are used interchangeably. More specifically, the report focuses on part-time and full-time students, young people and adults and those undertaking vocational as well as academic qualifications.

The report focuses on students in FEFC funded provision. It therefore excludes consideration of higher education students at further education (FE) colleges, although issues about funding in higher education are occasionally discussed. The report does, however, include individuals on government training programmes and those attending FE colleges who are sponsored by their employers. Individuals who are involved in employer-based training, or in private and voluntary sector training schemes, are not explicitly included.

1.4.2 Defining 'withdrawal'

The term 'drop-out' is habitually used in official statistics and institutional studies to describe any form of withdrawal before a course's anticipated date of completion. Other common terms are wastage, exits, attrition, withdrawal, non-persistence, non-continuation and non-completion. These terms can and are often defined in different ways (McGivney, 1996). In this study the term 'withdrawal', drop-out and non-completion are used. It is important for the reader to note that these terms are used to cover all aspects of not completing a course, including transfers, delayed completion as well as positive withdrawals.

1.5 METHODOLOGY

The research consisted exclusively of desk research. It involved:

- a variety of library searches at institutions such as the FEFC, Department for Education and Employment (DfEE), London School of Economics, and Institute of Education;
- explorations of a wide range of databases both in Britain and the United States, such as ERIC, PsychLit, EconLit, and SocioLit;
- some informal telephone interviews with representatives from a range of key organisations such as the Association of Colleges, charities, Institute of Education, DfEE, Inland Revenue, and the Unemployment Unit.

1.6 STRUCTURE OF THE REPORT

By way of setting the context for the discussion of financial support and its impact on participation, Chapter 2 focuses on the various sources of financial support available to students in further education. It highlights who, and how many individuals, are eligible for these different types of financial support and assesses the trends and developments in funding for students.

Chapter 3 discusses how there is a lack of research on financial support and participation, and why such work has been undertaken in the United States. It highlights some of the gaps and major limitations of research conducted in Britain.

Chapter 4 examines the issues of financial support and initial access. It explores the levels of participation; the non-financial factors affecting participation; and how financial support can act as an incentive and, conversely, how the lack of it works as a disincentive to participation. It draws on studies conducted both in Britain and the United States.

Chapter 5 focuses on the issues of financial support, retention and achievement. It considers the levels of retention and achievement; the non-financial factors affecting non-completion; and the extent to which financial support acts as an incentive to stay on and complete, and conversely, how the lack of it works as a disincentive. Again, it calls upon both British and American studies.

Chapter 6 is a critique of learning accounts which are one policy proposal aimed at tackling the issue of financial support and its associated problems described in Chapter 2.

The costs of further education and funding sources

2.1 INTRODUCTION

This chapter examines the nature and level of the costs involved in pursuing further education and the various sources of funding available to students. Each source of funding will be broadly discussed in terms of its origin; eligibility criteria; what it covers; the terms and conditions attached to it; the current take-up and penetration rate; changes over time with respect to take-up; current expenditure and changes over time and finally, the current value of payments and how they have changed over time. The final section of the chapter will assess the impact of these trends and developments in funding for students.

2.2 WHAT ARE THE COSTS OF FURTHER EDUCATION AND TRAINING?

Earlier work outlined the costs involved in pursing further education and training as primarily course fees and opportunity costs in terms of in time (Training Agency, 1989). But as De Bell and Davies (1991) have pointed out, 'the picture [is] more complex' (p109). The costs of education and training go beyond fees and opportunity costs and include a range of other indirect costs such as:

- add-on costs (for example, books, equipment, examination fees, registration fees)
- direct personal and family support costs while training (housing, food, living expenses)
- opportunity costs in foregone earnings
- childcare costs
- dependent relative care costs
- transport costs
- technical support aids, machinery adaptations and/or the training support costs needed by students with special needs.

No research exists which has attempted to quantify systematically these costs of participating in further education. However, research on the income and expenditure of higher education students (Callender and Kempson, 1996) shows that the expenditure of full-time undergraduates living at home was £3,466 for the 1995–96 academic year. Students spent an average of £506 on course-related items such as books and materials. Those who lived at home with their parents spent about £200 on travel to and from college.

The relative importance of each of these elements of cost tends to vary with changes in policy and the composition of the student body. For example, as steps are taken to widen participation in the sector and include non-traditional groups, costs associated with childcare and those particular to students with disabilities have assumed greater significance. Moreover, with the recent cuts in subsidised transport for students, travel costs are being emphasised (Page, 1996; Mansell, 1997).

There are also differences in the nature and extent of costs borne by different types of students. For example, adult students and especially women, are more likely than younger students to bear the range of personal and family support costs, dependent relative costs and childcare costs. Similarly, the issue of travel costs may be of greater significance to students living in rural areas who have to travel long distances to an educational institution, than to their counterparts living in the urban inner cities who may incur little, if any, travel costs.

The location, timing and duration of the course can also have cost implications for the student. For example, the full-time attendance requirement still in place on most Training and Enterprise Council (TEC) programmes may translate into a cost problem for students if transport and childcare are not fully funded. De Bell (1993) notes, however, that adult education services have been effective in reducing these costs by providing learning within community settings, and by using the full week, including evenings and weekends.

But the costs of further education and training are not always made explicit by providers to students. For example, in a recent FEU (1993) study of self-funded adult students in further education colleges, less than a quarter of the students in the sample (13 of the 57) thought that they were given adequate information about the costs before starting their respective courses. One student noted 'it sounded good at the interview when I was told there was no need to buy books. But there is a hidden outlay. Small things add up…' (p14). Indeed, Firth and Goffey (1996) in their study of learners' decision-making, found that it was only the more experienced learners who had considered the 'hidden costs' of learning such as books, photocopying, and stationery prior to taking up the course.

The increasing level of costs in further education is also of some concern. No research exists which has sought to quantify systematically the costs of participating in further education for different types of learners or how these costs may have changed over time. A few studies have, however, highlighted the increasing cost of certain aspects of further education. For example, local surveys in the late 1970s revealed that there were 'frequent and steep fee' increases (McGivney, 1990). More recently, there is growing evidence that fiscal pressures in the further education sector are increasing emphasis on income generation with resulting fee increases for individuals on some training courses, particularly those outside the FEFC umbrella (De Bell, 1993).

Mansell (1997) has also noted that the cost of books, accommodation and travel has risen. The latter has received particular attention. Whereas in the past travel costs were subsidised by LEAs, students are now facing higher charges. Under section 509 of the 1996 Local Education Authority Act, Local Education Authorities have a statutory duty to provide home-to-college travel assistance in certain circumstances and a discretionary power in others. So some students no longer receive help with their travel costs. Rising travel costs are a problem for young as well as adult students, rural as well as urban dwellers (Mansell, 1997).

These are just some of the ways in which the costs of further education have risen. They are important because they highlight the way in which costs may act as a barrier to participation in further education. However, it is not possible to ascertain the nature and extent of this problem without a deeper understanding of what funding is available and how this has changed over time. It is to these issues that we now turn.

2.3 WHAT ARE THE KEY FUNDING SOURCES?

2.3.1 Discretionary awards

Discretionary awards are made by Local Education Authorities (LEAs) directly to individuals under Section 2 of the 1962 Education Act. These awards are the main source of public funds for non-HE students in post-compulsory education aimed explicitly at meeting the costs of participation. Yet some authorities only make new awards exceptionally while others have cut provision by up to 50 per cent (NEAGA, 1994). Moreover, only a minority of all FE students receive them.

Of the three million students enrolled at colleges in the further education sector in England in 1994/95, only about 162,000 received discretionary awards – representing about one in twenty or 5 per cent of all FE students in England. By contrast, about three-quarters of all full-time students in higher education in the UK receive a mandatory grant from their local authority and about three out of five receive government subsidies through the receipt of student loans, irrespective of their financial need.[6]

Discretionary awards are paid entirely out of the Local Education Authority's (LEA) budget and there is no specific grant from central government. The local economic situation can therefore have considerable influence on discretionary awards policies. Indeed, since the early 1990s, discretionary award provision for students of further education has come under increasing pressure. A recent *Times Educational Supplement* article pointed out that

> …budgets are often provisional and subject to constant revision. Occasionally they are set in the knowledge that they are insufficient to meet demand. There are points systems, quotas and policies dictated by cash constraints rather than need. (Nash, 1994a, p11)

Overall, there has been a 10 per cent decline in expenditure on all further education discretionary awards since 1990. As indicated in Table 2.1, expenditure fell from £119 million in 1990/91 to £107.8 million in 1994/95. More recently, the decline in expenditure has been much greater. Since its peak in 1992/93, expenditure has fallen by a third. The number of people receiving awards peaked in 1993/94 but has since fallen to pre-1991/92 levels. As a result of these trends, the overall value of awards has fallen by 30 per cent since 1990/91 (Table 2.2).

In 1994/95 the average value of an award was £665, for the minority who received them. This sum is unlikely to be sufficient to meet the full costs of participation. By contrast, in 1995/96, the average value of a mandatory maintenance grant (excluding fees) for all full-time undergraduate HE students in the UK was £1,726 and £1,327 for those students living at home (Callender and Kempson, 1996). In addition, they could top up this grant with a student loan, the average value of which was £1,243.[7]

However, the discretionary nature of these awards for FE students means that the amount that an individual receives and what it covers varies enormously from one LEA to another. LEAs set their own policies regarding personal eligibility as well as the type of course and subject supported. They are also free to set their own policies about payments; they may only pay part of the fees and/or maintenance. Moreover, the rate at which these payments are made varies across authorities. For example, awards may be given as a percentage of the mandatory award maintenance rate or, alternatively, the LEA's own scale may be used. The latter itself varies from authority to authority, and may be lower or higher than that applicable for mandatory awards. Modest sums for students' course-related expenses such as equipment and field trips may also be provided (Eastwood and Casson, 1992; Fletcher-Campbell et al, 1994).

---

6   The current system of funding students in higher education is likely to change following the recommendations of the National Committee of Inquiry into Higher Education chaired by Sir Ron Dearing, and current government proposals.

7   For a more detailed analysis on the take-up of student loans, see Payne and Callender, 1997.

Table 2.1   Expenditure on Section 2 (FE) discretionary awards, England

						£ millions
	1990/91	1991/92	1992/93	1993/94	1994/95	% change 1992–1995
Fees and maintenance	119.6	150.9	156.4	133.0	107.8	-31
of which:						
16–18	–	–	36.5	48.2	45.6	+25
19+	–	–	119.9	84.7	61.9	-48

– data not available

Source: adapted from Table 3b in *Statistics for Education, Student Support, England and Wales 1994/95*, DfEE, 1996g

Expenditure on Section 2 (FE) discretionary awards

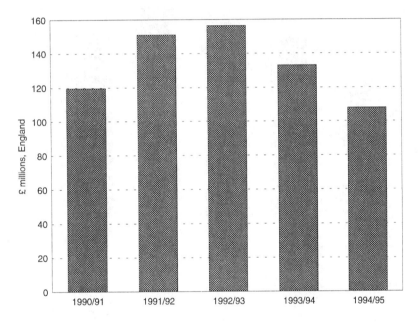

Source: DfEE, 1996g

The likelihood of receiving an award also depends on where the student lives. There are substantial differences between metropolitan and non-metropolitan authorities in the level of expenditure and number of awards granted. Expenditure on Section 2 (FE) awards by non-metropolitan authorities was estimated to have increased more between 1990/91 and 1992/93 (by 43 per cent) than in metropolitan authorities (by 16 per cent). There were also differences in the number of awards. Between 1990/91 and 1992/3 the number of discretionary awards made in non-metropolitan LEAs increased from approximately 80,000 to an estimated 125,000, while in metropolitan LEAs it fluctuated between 60,000 and 65,000 over the same period (Fletcher-Campbell et al, 1994).

Potential access to these awards also varies with the age of the student. Further analysis of the data on expenditure and the number of awards granted indicates that between 1992/93 and 1994/95 expenditure on discretionary awards to students between the ages of 16 and 18

Table 2.2   Number of Section 2 (FE) discretionary awards, England

	1990/91	1991/92	1992/93	1993/94	1994/95	*thousands* % change 1990–1995
All discretionary awards *of which:*	129.2	165.8	175.0	187.6	161.9	+25
16–18				110.6	112.6	
19+				77.0	49.3	

Source: adapted from Table 2b in *Statistics for Education, Student Support, England and Wales 1994/95*, DfEE, 1996g

Number of Section 2 (FE) discretionary awards

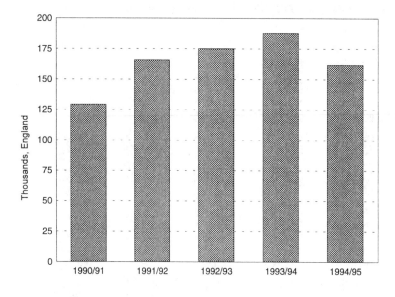

Source: DfEE, 1996g

increased by 25 per cent, while that for students aged 19 and over was almost halved. Similarly, the proportion of grants to younger students increased over the same period while that for older students declined by one fifth (see Table 2.3). But it is important to set this in context. These changes are taking place at a time when an increasing number of students coming into the sector are over the age of 19.

The discretionary nature of these awards also extends to the type of course pursued. For example, the National Conference of Drama Schools has reported that the number of local authorities willing to provide full discretionary awards for drama students has fallen from 83 per cent in 1987 to 34 per cent in 1994 (Charter, 1995, TES). A more recent article by Hinds (1997) reiterated this point. He argued that the lack of discretionary grants is threatening the future of British dance and drama training.

Table 2.3   Proportion of expenditure in Section 2 (FE) discretionary awards by age, England

£ millions

	1992/93	1993/94	1994/95
16–18	23.3	36.2	42.5
19+	76.7	63.7	57.4

Source: adapted from Table 3b in *Statistics for Education, Student Support, England and Wales 1994/95*, DfEE, 199g6

In discussing the implications of two recent court decisions on discretionary awards, Diamond concluded that 'the decisions have given LEAs a (virtual) unfettered discretion in the number of such awards to be made, the class of the student entitled to such awards and in the allocation of budgetary awards to such students' (Diamond, 1996, p61).

To conclude, the system of discretionary awards has become a lottery. The receipt of awards is dependent on where the student lives or what they study rather than on their financial need or even academic merit. There are no guarantees that a student will receive any funds from this source.

In addition to these discretionary awards, under Section 509 of the 1996 Local Education Authority Act, LEAs have a statutory duty to provide home-to-college travel assistance in certain circumstances and a discretionary power in others. This legislation marks a change in the thrust of previous policies and as a result fewer students now receive financial help with their travel costs. And like discretionary awards, the receipt of travel assistance can depend as much on where students live, as their need for such support.

2.3.2   Access and Hardship funds

Access funds were introduced by the government in 1990/91, for students aged 19 and over, to provide discretionary support for individual cases of hardship or where financial considerations may inhibit access to further or higher education (DfEE, 1996e).

The FE sector is allocated about 20 per cent of the total government budget on Access funds. In 1995/96, this allocation stood at £6 million. The remainder goes to HE. This is despite the fact that a much higher proportion of students in FE than HE come from low social economic groups and thus a higher proportion have a need for financial help. And despite the fact that most HE students, unlike FE students, are eligible for some state-funded financial support.

In 1995/96 46,872 students in the FE sector in England received Access funds, of which 42,249 were FE students[8] – about 1.5 per cent of all students in the sector. They received on average £96. By contrast, in 1995/96 5 per cent of full-time undergraduates in the UK gained money from Access funds and the average amount they received was three times greater – £358[9] (Callender and Kempson, 1996). Between 1994/95 and 1995/96, 27 per cent more students received Access funds but they received on average 10 per cent less money.

Access funds, like discretionary awards, are a lottery. They too are highly discretionary. Individual educational institutions are free to set their own criteria for considering applications within guidelines set down by the DfEE. Though these funds were not set up to replace state social security benefits no longer available to students, in practice these institutions may allocate funds where benefits are no longer available. Indeed, policy in

---

8   4,512 students in the sector receiving Access funds were doing HE courses and 115 were following postgraduate courses.

9   This figure includes money received from both their institutions' Access and Hardship funds.

Table 2.4   Use of access funds in further education, 1995/96, England

	No. of students in the FE sector	Total expenditure (£)	Amount per student (£)	% of total expenditure
Fees	7,486	957,463	128	15
Books	11,291	448,158	40	7
Equipment	10,831	664,391	61	11
Accommodation	3,146	405,259	129	7
Childcare	5,784	1,397,249	242	22
Transport	18,378	1,657,554	90	27
Other	8,043	681,620	85	11
Total	**64,959***	**6,211,694**	**96**	**100**

*   Some students receive assistance under more than one category

Source: FEFC, 1997, unpublished data

Use of access funds in further education, 1994/95, England

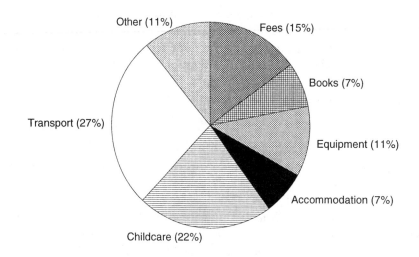

Source: FEFC, 1997, unpublished data

allocating funding seems to vary from best practice – targeting those with greatest need but with little chance of getting support from elsewhere, to worst practice – simply dividing the total available by the number of eligible applicants, thereby ensuring that everyone eligible receives at least £1 per week irrespective of relative need (Eastwood and Casson, 1992).

Educational institutions allocate these funds to cover a range of direct and indirect costs. As Table 2.4 shows, in 1995/96 Access funds were used predominantly to fund travel and childcare costs as well as fees. Per capita expenditure on childcare was highest followed by accommodation and fees. Together these three elements of cost consumed almost two-thirds of the budget. However, the level of support received by students on average is low and do not meet the full costs of participation.

In addition to the funds received from central government to aid students in financial difficulties, most FE colleges have Hardship funds, some devoting as much as 3–4 per cent of their annual budgets to these funds (Cantor et al, 1995). No national data, however, are available on the overall expenditure or the total number of beneficiaries. Funds are raised through a number of college initiatives including seeking contributions from, for example, local businesses. Indeed, the 'pot of money' available depends on a number of factors including the fund raising capacity of the individual college. This source of financial support is also highly discretionary as it is cash limited and highly competitive – demand often times outweighing supply.

2.3.3   Fee remission

Fee remission is a very important indirect form of financial support. However, it is an indirect payment and does not go to students directly, unlike grants and Access funds. All young people under the age of 19 years in further education do not have to pay tuition fees. In addition, certain groups of people on low incomes are exempt from paying fees. These include:

- unemployed people in receipt of Job Seekers' Allowance (JSA) and their unwaged dependants
- those in receipt of means-tested benefit and their unwaged dependants
- those taking programmes where the primary goal is adult basic education or English for speakers of other languages.

The number of Council-funded students in sector colleges who received fee remissions in 1995/96 stood at almost 1.3 million which represents about a third of all further education students (FEFC, unpublished data, 1997). Most students had their fees remitted for 'other reasons' rather than because they were in receipt of social security benefits.

Since incorporation, remission policies have been set nationally by the FEFC rather than by individual LEAs. Thus a significant source of unequal treatment has been eradicated but the policy remains selective. Moreover, this fee remission policy does not address the costs of living and other expenses such as examination fees, books and materials and travel which are incurred whilst undertaking the course (Uden, 1994; Donnelly, 1997). In addition, there are some groups, outside the means-tested benefit categories, who may also be unable to meet fees and other costs. These include low-waged workers and their dependants, certain people with disabilities and learning difficulties who receive non-tested benefits (Uden, 1994).

2.3.4   TEC funding

Since their inception in 1990, Training and Enterprise Councils, they have been responsible for delivering and developing the Government's training and enterprise programmes in England and Wales. They usually do not provide training directly but make contracts with local providers such as colleges, private training institutions and employers. They are also responsible for the administration of the training credit scheme and for meeting the National Education and Training Targets (NETTs).[10] TECs are responsible for government training programmes, the most significant of which are Youth Training (YT) and Training for Work (TfW).

---

10   The NETTs aim to improve the UK's international competitiveness by raising standards and attainment in education and training to world-class levels.

Youth Training

In 1995/96, 251,000 young people in England started on a Youth Training (YT) programme and 25,900 started on the Modern Apprenticeships programme. Youth Training (YT), introduced in 1990, is targeted primarily at 16–17 year olds. Indeed, the government guarantees the offer of a YT place for all 16–17 year olds who are not in full-time education or a job and are seeking training. This guarantee can be extended to 18 year olds and over who have been prevented from completing or taking up YT for a variety of reasons.[11] YT programmes can last up to two years and they offer participants the opportunity to receive training and work experience leading to a recognised vocational qualification. Expenditure on this programme was £718 million in 1990/91, and the forecast expenditure in 1996/97 is £721 million (DfEE, 1996a).

Participants have their main training costs covered via their local TEC, including add-on costs. Sometimes their transport costs are also covered – but this is at the TEC's discretion. In addition, they receive a training allowance and/or a wage. In April 1997 the YT allowance for 16 year olds was increased by 50p to £30 a week while the amount for 17–18 year olds has remained the same at £35. Participants are guaranteed funding, but the allowances for the older participants have been frozen since the late 1980s. They have not kept pace with inflation and some of the rates have been lower than Income Support rates, which brings into question their effectiveness as incentives for people to enter training. Indeed, the recent rise in the rate for 16 year olds was to stay ahead of Income Support rates. Moreover, there is an element of lottery in terms of the money they receive. Some employers and training providers are paying higher than the minimum training allowance, but about a third of those on YT get only the minimum rate.

Training for Work

Training for Work (TfW) is the main route open to the adult unemployed wishing to gain a qualification. This programme aims to help them find jobs and to improve their work-related skills. The combination of activities offered include:

- training;
- temporary work
- work towards vocational qualifications;
- job-specific training and work preparation according to the needs of the individual and their local labour market.

Since its inception in 1993, the number of participants on TfW schemes has been falling. In March 1994, 124,000 people in England were in training, but by March 1996 this had halved to 69,000. In recent years the budget has also been drastically cut. For example, the amount of money allocated to this programme has fallen from £541 million in 1995/96 to a planned expenditure of £451 in 1997/98 (Donnelly, 1997).

Like YT, TfW covers the key course costs. Participants get their social security benefits plus a £10 weekly top-up. This top-up has remained the same since 1986 and does not cover all the add-on costs associated with training.

Participants receive travel expenses and living away from home allowance which does not affect the amount of benefit they receive. Some can also get allowances to meet the cost of childcare. However, these allowances are discretionary and benefit only certain groups of women. A recent small-scale survey of TECs and training providers found that only 3 per cent of women trainees obtained childcare allowances (McQuail, 1993 in Callender and

---

11   These reasons include disability, ill health, pregnancy, custodial sentence, remand in custody, language difficulties or as a result of a care order.

Metcalf, 1997). Moreover, both the level of the allowance and the eligibility criteria are at the discretion of the TEC and the provider. Providers also vary in their commitment and ability to support trainees with childcare costs. Indeed, some have ceased paying childcare allowances (De Bell, 1993).

According to Donnelly (1997), TfW is failing to meet the expectations of the unemployed or the aims of the National Education and Training Targets (NETTS). She points out that 52 per cent of those leaving TfW in 1995/96 did not gain a qualification while only 41 per cent of leavers obtained a full qualification. As significant is the way the emphasis of the programme has changed from one of obtaining qualifications to job outcomes. Indeed, the percentage of TfW leavers projected by the DfEE to gain NVQs was reduced from 41 per cent in 1994/95 to 30 per cent in 1997/98, although the actual performance may be higher. According to Donnelly (1997), given these shifts it is not surprising that unemployed people are turning to colleges and other providers to gain the skills and qualifications they want.

2.3.5   Social security

Social security benefits are another essential source of financial support for an estimated 100,000 unemployed individuals in the FE sector. Prior to the introduction of the Job Seekers Allowance (JSA), people receiving Unemployment Benefit (UB) or Income Support (IS) because they were unemployed could undertake part-time education and training, as long as they remained available for and actively seeking work. Claimants could train or study for 21 hours without affecting their benefit. This was the so-called '21 hour rule.'

In October 1996, JSA replaced Income Support (IS) and Unemployment Benefit (UB) for people who have to sign on as available for work. It allows claimants to take up part-time education or training while looking for work as long as s/he:

- is a part-time student;
- is available to start work immediately;
- is willing/able to take time off the course to attend a job interview;
- can be contacted promptly while attending the course;
- can rearrange the hours of the course to fit around a job or is prepared to abandon the course at once in order to take up a job of over 24 hours per week.

Failure to satisfy these conditions can result in benefit being suspended and being referred to an adjudication officer or withdrawn. These rules on education and training while receiving JSA are largely carried forward from the previous system. However, three main changes were brought in by the JSA.

First, definitions of full-time and part-time are now provided. Courses funded by the FEFC are defined as part-time if they consist of no more than 16 guided learning hours a week. Under the previous system, there was no definition in law of full-time and part-time education and training. However, it was widely believed that the definition of part-time was education and training of no more than 21 hours a week.

Second, a new concession, Regulation 11 was introduced. This concession is intended to make it easier for unemployed students or trainees to meet the requirement to be available for work. According to Regulation 11, in determining whether a claimant is available for employment, no matter relating to the course of study shall be relevant provided that the claimant:

- is part-time;
- is willing and able to rearrange the hours of the course in order to take up employment within his/her pattern of availability and to take up such employment immediately;
- has been in receipt of JSA, Incapacity Benefit or IS because they are sick or disabled or has been on a Government employment or training programme for a period of three

months immediately prior to the course starting or for a total of three months out of the previous six months if s/he was working temporarily in between (Donnelly, 1996a).

Third, people receiving JSA can undertake one employment related course of education or training of no more than two weeks in any year with the agreement of the Employment Service and meanwhile be excused from the requirements to be available for and actively seeking work (DfEE, 1997).

The exact number of unemployed people affected by these part-time study rules is unknown. The Government has estimated that 80,000 people are affected. However, the results of research carried out by the Association for Colleges in April 1995, found that the figure was 'well in excess of 100,000' (AfC, 1995, in Donnelly, 1997).

Recent research carried out by the Unemployment Unit among 19 further education colleges in London gave some indication as to why the exact figure is not known. Colleges do not routinely collect information about the number of unemployed students: they are not obliged to do so for funding purposes. Some colleges make estimates using the FEFC fee waiver categories. However, these categories only specify if the student is in receipt of Unemployment Benefit or Income Support and not the *reason* for receiving Income Support. Indeed, claimants of Income Support may not necessarily be unemployed; they could be claiming as lone parents or disabled students. These groups are covered by a different set of rules.

Whatever the exact figure, many commentators do not believe the government's claim that, with the introduction of JSA, 'broadly the same numbers of unemployed people will be able to study part-time as now' (quoted in Donnelly, 1996b, p18). For example, Garner and Imeson (1996) drawing from their survey of 58 Access tutors in Greater London and the South East, found that over 70 per cent of their respondents felt that students would have to make a choice between benefit and study. This, in turn, would affect recruitment leading to a major reduction in student numbers.

However, the new regulations may have other consequences. Almost 60 per cent of respondents in the Unemployment Unit's research believed that the 16 hour limit would have a negative effect on course content (Donnelly, 1996b). Tutors in the survey conducted by Garner and Imeson (1996) came to a similar conclusion. There is also some concern that cuts to ensure that programmes stay within the limit may discriminate against certain groups of students. For example, any cuts in additional support in the form of help with literacy and numeracy would disproportionately affect students with those needs, many of whom may already have been passed over by the school system (Donnelly, 1996b).

Perhaps most important of all, for this study, is the likely impact of the 16 hour rule on drop-out. In the Unemployment Unit's research 'the majority of responding colleges felt that the 16 hour limit would increase drop-out, adversely affect college funding and jeopardise student achievement' (Donnelly, 1996b, p18).

Research into the operation of the 21 hour rule showed that there was widespread inconsistency in its application by different benefit officers and different members of staff (Donnelly, 1996b; Finn, 1995; Garner and Imeson, 1996). It is still too early to tell whether or not the new 16 hour rule will be applied more equitably. However, even if the rule were applied more consistently, the basic premise of the rules remains the same: unemployed claimants who undertake training or a course of study must be 'available for' and 'actively seeking' employment. This entails undergoing constant scrutiny and testing and demonstrating a lack of commitment to the course (Donnelly, 1996b). Indeed, under JSA, compulsion has been stepped up. Claimants are expected to attend more interviews and to participate in more government schemes under the threat of benefit sanction; a situation which can prove to be highly disruptive (Hyde, 1992; Donnelly, 1997).[12]

---

12 In April 1997 'Workskill Pilot' schemes were introduced in four areas in the country to test whether more flexible study rules would improve the employment prospects of unemployed people.

In addition to these problems, the actual benefit levels are low. Students often find it difficult to cope. They often have to borrow from friends and family to top up benefit because they do not receive any additional premiums or benefits to cover the cost of the course. The amount they receive is governed by JSA regulations and depends on their individual circumstances. For example, at the time of writing, a single person, over the age of 25 receives £47 per week in JSA.

In drawing his conclusions about the possible implications of the JSA, Finn (1995, pp1–2) commented that:

> the JSA legislation offered a significant opportunity to simplify the complex and contradictory rules which both limit the study opportunities of the unemployed and make course planning for providers so difficult Unfortunately, the proposed reduction of existing rules are already limiting and reducing opportunities.

To conclude, there is nothing secure about this source of funding. Students may have to stop studying to protect their benefit entitlement. The rules act as a major disincentive to study among a particularly vulnerable group who are especially likely to benefit from access to education and training. Yet again, like other sources of funding, there is an element of a lottery at play. The extent to which colleges can be flexible in their provision to allow claimants to continue with courses, if they start work, varies depending on the college and the course. Perhaps more important, the rules are so complicated and confusing that, in practice, they may not be operated consistently either by Employment Service offices or by colleges across the country.

Benefit, training and young people

All young people under the age of 19 are entitled to 'free' full-time education. In other words, their fees are paid, but no additional costs are covered. It is assumed that parents will incur any direct personal costs associated with full-time study. Their parents receive Child Benefit in respect of them; the young people themselves are not entitled to benefit in their own right.

Young people, under the age of 19 in full time non-advanced education can receive Income Support in their own right under certain restricted circumstances. These include:

- lone parents;
- people with severe mental or physical disabilities who would have difficulty getting work because of that disability;
- orphans who do not have anyone else acting in place of their parents;
- those who have to live away from their parents (or those acting as parents) because of estrangement, physical or moral danger or a serious risk to physical or mental health;
- those living away from their parents (or those acting as parents) because the parents cannot support the young person financially and they (the parents) are chronically sick or disabled, or in prison or prohibited from entering the UK;
- refugees who are not required to be available for work.

It is important to note that lone parents and students with disabilities can continue to receive Income Support when they reach their 19th birthday, regardless of the level of course that they are pursuing.

Moreover, 16–17 year olds who are not unemployed and not in full-time education are not normally entitled to benefit but are guaranteed a Youth Training place with an allowance. In exceptional circumstances, certain 16–17 year olds who are unemployed and not in full-time education are, however, entitled to JSA while they look for a Youth Training place or work (DfEE, 1997)

2.3.6   The European Social Fund

The European Social Fund (ESF) pays for the unemployed and socially disadvantaged groups such as migrants and refugees to participate in education and training. However, not all colleges apply for or succeed in accessing these funds. They have to compete for funds with TECs, higher education institutions, and the voluntary sector. In 1993, 60 per cent of colleges received funding from the ESF (Jones, 1994). In 1995, 120,000 students in the sector benefited from ESF funded programmes, up from 110,000 in 1994 (DfEE fax, 20 February 1997).

The majority of ESF funding (for Objective 3), however, is allocated to central government. The FE sector gets about a sixth of all allocations. In 1994 allocations to the further education sector in England stood at £36 million, and increased to over £63 million[13] by 1996. Therefore, given the policy of 45:55 matching funding, this resulted in £79 million to £140 million worth of training.

For students enrolled on ESF funded courses at colleges, fees and other educational costs are covered. Unlike their counterparts on TfW programmes, they do not usually receive a training allowance. However, parents of young children are often, but not always, entitled to free childcare. Colleges are reimbursed at the rate of £50 per student to cover the cost of provision. Unemployed people participating in these courses at colleges continue to be supported by the benefit system. In contrast, individuals on ESF funded courses in the voluntary sector often receive training allowances, free transport, and other payments in kind such as free meal vouchers.

2.3.7   Career Development Loans

Career Development Loans (CDLs) have been available since 1988 to students who want to follow a course which is relevant to employment. The course does not have to lead to a recognised qualification and can either be part-time or full-time, and institution-based or by distance learning. Support is usually for a maximum of two years. With the introduction of the CDL Plus pilot scheme the loan period has been expanded to last three years, to cover two years of training plus one year of practical experience.

The personal eligibility criteria for these loans are well defined. The individual must be aged 18 or over on the day that the loan starts; employed, self-employed, unemployed, student or returning to work after a period of non-employment; not in receipt of a Local Authority Mandatory Grant; not in receipt of other funding which covers the expenses applied for through the CDL; intend to work in the UK or elsewhere in the EU.

Loans between £200 and £8,000 are available to pay for up to 80 per cent of course fees. Applicants who have been out of work for at least three months at the time of the application can apply for a loan to cover 100 per cent of the course fees, provided that their local TEC endorses the application. Living expenses can be considered for full-time students. In 1995/96, the total value of loans approved under the scheme was £47 million (DfEE, 1996f). There has been a steady increase both in the total expenditure and the average amount of loans since 1991/92 (DfEE, 1992; DfEE, 1993; DfEE,1994; DfEE, 1995).

CDLs operate in partnership between the DfEE and four high-street banks. No repayments are required during the training period and up to one month afterwards. People registered unemployed at the time that the payments should start can apply to defer payments for up to an additional five months. During the deferred repayment period the Department pays the interest on the loan. It is then up to the borrower to repay the loan and the further interest over the length of time agreed with the bank concerned. The interest on CDLs is at commercial rates.

---

13   This is a committed allocation and may well change.

The total[14] take-up of CDLs has been low and disappointing. For example, in mid 1993 the Employment Department announced that 'significant expansion is planned over the next four years, rising from a capacity of 30,000 loans in 1993/94 to 52,000 by 1996/97' (CDL Annual Report 1992/93, ED, July 1995). By 1994/95, the target had been reduced to 20,000 but even then CDLs underperformed with only 15,000 loans being taken out (Donnelly, 1997). In the first nine months of 1996/97, just over 9,000 loans had been approved (House of Commons Hansard Written Answers, 30 January 1997), which if extrapolated, will result in an annual decline of over 1,000 from the 1995/96 figure of 13,000. Indeed, this decline takes into account the 173 loans taken out under the CDL Plus pilot scheme in which people are allowed to defer repayment of a loan for 18 months instead of six months under the standard CDL (Donnelly, 1997).

Research carried out by the Employment Department, before the introduction of the CDL Plus pilot scheme, indicated that this resistance may be due to financial prudence on the part of the unemployed and other target groups. It found that, while CDLs have helped some self-funding learners, the prospect of taking out a loan ('adding to debt') is very unattractive to many people whose economic circumstances may already be damaged by unemployment and other changes which have triggered the need for learning (ED, 1995). In 1996/97, 42 per cent of loan recipients were women. The relatively lower take-up of CDLs by women has also been explained in similar terms. It is believed that women are reluctant to saddle their families with debt and are aware of their limited salary and employment possibilities (Payne, 1991). Moreover, recent research on the take-up of student loans demonstrates a similar resistance among women undergraduates (Payne and Callender, 1997).

Indeed, this fear of falling into debt may be well founded. Data from 1993/94 show that the banks are taking action against more than 150 people a month for failing to repay their loans. Since 1988, action has been taken against 5,000 people (10 per cent of CDL trainees) for unrecovered loans totalling over £4 million. A third of those defaulting have failed to find a job (Murray, 1996).

Moreover, it appears that CDLs have not been particularly successful in promoting participation in further education and training. The evidence suggests that, in fact, they are fast becoming a vehicle for graduates to finance postgraduate courses and are not promoting the range of vocational training as originally planned. For example, in 1993/94, 45 per cent of trainees used CDLs for university courses, up from 17 per cent the previous year while only 6 per cent used them to acquire NVQs. The funding of higher education courses not covered by public grants, particularly at postgraduate level, is becoming a significant element of CDLs (Murray, 1996).

2.3.8   Tax relief

The Vocational Tax Relief (VTR), which was introduced in 1992, offers tax relief to an individual who is paying for his/her own vocational training provided that s/he is:

- a resident of the United Kingdom for tax purposes
- not receiving or entitled to receive financial assistance for a course under any of the following government schemes:
  - Youth Training
  - Employment Training
  - Employment Action
  - Training Credits
  - Career Development Loans and top-up payments made by the DTI's Inner Cities Task Force Schemes

---

14   Data on take-up of CDLs to pursue further education are not available.

      – mandatory award
      – local education authority discretionary awards
      – student loans
      – college Access funds
      – assistance from overseas public funds

- not entitled to any other tax relief in respect of the payment.

Moreover, VTR applies to training which is capable of counting towards a National Vocational Qualification (NVQ), and to full-time vocational courses lasting at least four weeks and up to one year, whether or not this is linked to an NVQ. The relief does not apply to general educational qualifications such as GCSEs or A levels, even when these are taken as a preliminary to NVQ study (Manson-Smith, 1993).

VTR is available to taxpayers and non-taxpayers, and is given by deduction of basic rate tax from payments made for training. Relief at the higher rate of tax is given by the tax office (Manson-Smith, 1993). Since its introduction, the amount claimed has increased sixfold – from £5 million in 1992/3 to an estimated £30 million in 1996/97 (Wilson, 1996). Tax relief is given on:

- study, examination and registration fees;
- fees payable for assessment purposes, including assessment of prior learning;
- payment for any award or certificate obtained;
- payment for entry in an official register such as the National Record of Achievement.

Where the cost of a course includes the cost of books or equipment together with study fees, only the fees are eligible for relief. However, the cost of materials, printed, audio or video, essential to training which are provided by the training organisation and are not generally available commercially, qualifies for relief. Relief is not given on payments for equipment or textbooks or the cost of travelling or subsistence in connection with the training (Manson-Smith, 1993).

VTR is a useful concession for self-funded students, but it helps only a minority. The tax credit is paid directly to the training provider so people still need access to funds or credit to pay for fees, even if those fees are reduced. Those really in need of help are unlikely to have well-paid jobs or be able to pay the reduced education and training fees upfront (Hyde, 1992).

In addition to this new relief for vocational training, there are two extra-statutory concessions which give limited relief for training costs. However, relief under these concessions is not available where VTR is due.

The first of these extra-statutory concessions (Extra-statutory Concession A64) applies where an employee attends an external training course relating to his/her employment, and incurs expenses in attending which are not reimbursed by his/her employer. This type of relief is given where all of the following conditions are met:

- the employee continues to receive his/her salary from the employer during the course but is allowed time off to attend it during normal working hours;
- the course is one which the employee is required or encouraged to attend by his/her employer with the view to increasing his/her effectiveness in the performance of present or prospective duties in that employment;
- the course is full-time requiring the employee's attendance on every or virtually every working day for four consecutive weeks or more;
- the course takes place in the UK;
- the expenses do not relate to a resit course or examination.

The course need not lead to a qualification.

Tax relief is available to employees on their fees, essential books and additional travel or living expenses when it is necessary to be away temporarily from the normal place of work. It is believed that the criteria attached to this concession are so restrictive that very few professional people are likely to gain any benefit.

The take-up and amount claimed in relief are not monitored by the Inland Revenue, but it is estimated that it amounts to about £500 million per year (Barlow, personal communication, April 1997).

The second concession (Extra-statutory Concession A63) relates to external training courses where expenses are borne or reimbursed by the employer. Such expenses could be treated as additional income to the employee, and thus be liable to income tax. Provided, however, that the training leads to the acquisition of skills or knowledge necessary for the performance of duties of employment, or is directly related to increasing the employee's present or prospective employment, the expenses are not charged to tax (Manson-Smith, 1993). This concession is also not monitored but the amount claimed is believed to be relatively small (Barlow, personal communication, April 1997).

2.3.9 Employers

Employers are another very important source of financial support for those participating in further education. Recent data on the number of employer-sponsored students in the further education sector are not readily available. Those that are show that the number of employer-led part-time enrolments in FE colleges fell by 16 per cent between 1988 and 1993 to 305,000, and this fall was much greater for 16–18 year olds (Rowlingson, 1996).

Employer-funded training tends to cover, at a minimum, maintenance for the student through the payment of wages while pursuing training. Support for the other associated costs such as fees, books and materials, transport and childcare is given at the discretion of individual employers. A recent study of individuals' take-up of NVQs, found that of those employees who were given time off work to do their qualification, 93 per cent were given *paid* time off. Further, two-thirds of all employees received other types of help from their employers. This included paying towards their course/registration fees, received by two-thirds; the costs of books, materials or equipment (20 per cent); their travel expenses for attending the course (12 per cent) Callender (1997b). Another recent study of part-time students in higher education revealed that of those that were employed, a half had all or part of their fees paid for them by their employer and two-fifths had been given paid time off work to pursue their studies (Callender, 1997a).

The support for training, however, is not uniform among employers. In a recent study, for example, De Bell (1993) found instances where, although the employees were prepared to pay for their own training, their paths were blocked by employers' refusal to release them for training; neither direct financial support nor support in terms of time-off or flexible working arrangements was granted. In those instances, the rigidity of the employers' work patterns conflicted with the rigidity of course provision and consequently employees lose out (De Bell, 1993).

Even where employer support is forthcoming, it is well established that not all employees have equal access to training (Gallie and White, 1993). Those most disadvantaged in the labour market, have the least access. Hence, women, part-time and contract workers, less qualified workers as well as younger employees tend to have fewer training opportunities; the odds favour employees in well-paid jobs higher up the occupational ladder.

2.3.10 Charities

In the early 1990s, there were reports of growing numbers of further education students turning to charities for financial support, particularly to pay fees. Though there was a lack of statistical evidence to substantiate these claims, there was 'clear anecdotal evidence that trusts were getting more and more applications from students...' (Maxwell, 1994 TES). For example, Richmond Parish Lands Charity reported the numbers applying as 'virtually exhaustive' while the Sheila Kay Fund in Liverpool, which helps women returners to education in poor areas in Merseyside, agreed that their outlay had increased by more than 300 per cent in three years (since 1991) (Maxwell, 1994 TES). Similar sentiments were also expressed by the Sir John Cass Foundation (Sir John Cass Foundation, 1994). This trend was believed to be linked to the cuts in the number and value of discretionary awards made at that time. Indeed, the increasing demand on the Sir John Cass Foundation propelled them to mount a study on the status of discretionary awards in England and Wales.

However, since the mid-1990s, the situation seems to have changed. Discussions with administrators at a few education charities during the course of this research revealed that the demand on charities has actually fallen in recent years. For example, for the past two years Skinner's Company has underspent its budget (Barlow, personal communication, February 1997). The Sir John Cass Foundation also reported a fall in demand from further education students (Brenner, personal communication, February 1997). The charities are unclear about the reasons for this reversal, but it is believed that the more liberal fee remission policies of the FEFC and colleges since 1994 may be an important contributory factor. Another factor may be that people have been put off from applying to charities because they were over-subscribed in the past. At the same time, some charities have tightened their eligibility criteria (Brenner, personal communication, February 1997).

Moreover, the type of people most in need of financial help and the nature of costs needing covering are changing, and charities are unable to respond due to the conditions attached to their respective charters. For example, the results of a small-scale telephone survey conducted by the Sir John Cass Foundation indicated that refugees were among the neediest groups and that childcare costs were a major barrier to participation. However, the Foundation is unable to respond to this group or to cover this cost since it is not within its remit to do so. An upshot of these changes is that the Foundation is now increasingly funding postgraduate students (Brenner, personal communication, February 1997).

2.4 WHAT ARE THE TRENDS AND DEVELOPMENTS IN FUNDING FOR LEARNERS?

Further education students, then, fund their participation through a combination of benefits, grants and in some cases earnings. There is no comprehensive system of funding students in this sector; funding is obtained from a variety of sources, mainly from government (Table 2.5). This approach is distinctive, particularly when compared to the situation which obtains in the higher education sector. Nearly all higher education students get their fees paid and approximately 70 per cent of them receive some form of maintenance grant. Yet students in higher education tend to come from a higher socio-economic class background compared to their counterparts in further education, and the financial returns to higher education are likely to be higher than that from further education and training.[15]

Moreover, not only is there little or no guaranteed minimum financial support for further education students, particularly adults, but recent years have witnessed a decline in the amount of funds and the value of the awards available from these discretionary sources. This has certainly been the case with discretionary awards, a major source of funding for further education students. Superimposed upon this is the increasing tendency to tighten eligibility criteria, making funding increasingly discretionary.

---

15   The funding of students in higher education is currently under review.

Table 2.5   Origin of the various sources of funding

	Government	Private sector inc. voluntary sector	Employers	College	European Union
Discretionary grants	●				
Access funds	●				
Hardship funds				●	
Fee remission	●				
TECs	●				●
Social security	●				
European Social Fund					●
Career Development Loans		●			
Tax relief	●				
Employers			●		
Charities		●			

There are also wide variations in the eligibility criteria for certain sources of financial support. In some instances, eligibility varies with place of residence, as in the case of discretionary awards, while in others, it varies with the college attended such as in Access funds. Or even, as in the case of social security benefits, with the interpretation of the rules by a particular benefits officer or member of college staff. The operation of the system in this way introduces the elements of 'luck and chance' and raises questions of equality and the equity of access to funding, and consequently to further education and training itself.

But what have been the implications of these changes and developments for the different groups of students? Those students, both young people and adults, who are on government training schemes, are fully supported and this support is not discretionary. But the similarities between these two groups end there. Younger students, specifically those in full-time further education are at least entitled to fee remission; there are no such guarantees for adult students (see Table 2.6). Adults are having to depend on the range of discretionary sources of support which are localised, variable and falling in value.

Moreover, there is uneven coverage of the costs incurred in pursuing further education by the sources of support available. As indicated in Table 2.7, coverage is best for tuition fees but worse for meals, maintenance of the student and his/her dependants. The latter would

Table 2.6   Sources a of funding and types of students

	16–19 full time	16–19 YT	16–19 unsupported	Over 19 full-time	TfW	Unemployed	Employed supported	Employed unsupported
Discretionary grants	●		●	●				
Access funds				●		●		●
Hardship funds	●		●	●		●		●
Fee remission	●		●	●		●		●
TECs		●			●	●		●
Social security	●		●			●		
European Social Fund	●			●		●		
Career Development Loans	●			●	●			●
Tax relief							●	●
Employers							●	
Charities	●		●	●		●		●

Table 2.7 Each source of funding and what it covers

	Transport	Child-care	Tuition	Regist-ration fees	Books, equipment, materials	Exam fees	Meals	Mainte-nance for students
Discretionary grants			●			●		●
Access funds	●	●			●	●	●	●
Hardship funds	●	●	●	●	●	●	●	
Fee remission			●					
TECs	●	●	●	●	●	●		
Social security								●
European Social Fund	●	●	●	●	●	●	●	
Career Development Loans			●					
Tax relief			●	●		●		
Employers	●	●	●	●	●	●	●	●
Charities			●					

disproportionately affect adult students. The coverage for the other associated costs such as childcare, transport, books and registration fees fall between these two extremes. But one would be misguided to think that these are on an equal footing. Support for transport, for example, is diminishing. Moreover, the level of costs involved are also different. The cost of adequate childcare, for example, is much higher than that incurred in registration and exam fees.

2.5 SUMMARY

The costs of further education and training are rising. They are also becoming more varied as the student population changes. At the same time, the financial support framework for students is breaking down. There is no comprehensive or universal system of financial support for individuals in further education, unlike provisions for full-time students in higher education. Students in FE are the 'poor relation' of these HE students in terms of access to funding, and the type and level of financial support available. This is despite the fact that their financial need is likely to be greater, given their socio-economic characteristics. The current funding system of further and higher education favours young, full-time, academic learners while penalising adult, part-time and vocationally orientated and focused learners.

Students are having to fund their education and training from a variety of sources, many of which are localised, highly discretionary, variable and time-consuming to claim. They are increasingly having to shoulder the financial burdens of education and training themselves. If participation in the sector is to be widened, then funding policies need to consider not just the direct educational costs such as fees and books, but also the other cost barriers which may inhibit the participation of many non-traditional groups such as lone parents. Moreover, there is a need for a more consistent, reliable, equitable and less anomalous approach to funding further education.

Chapter 3

Researching the role of financial support

3.1 INTRODUCTION

Overall, relatively little research has been conducted on the impact of financial support on participation in further education in Britain, unlike in the United States. Moreover, the research which has been conducted in Britain is limited, which brings into question its robustness and accuracy. This chapter discusses, therefore, the development of research in the United States: it aims to form a context for understanding the research reported on in the two following chapters and to locate policy developments in student finance within the United States. The chapter also highlights some of the gaps and major drawbacks of the research conducted in Britain and forms an important backdrop and context for understanding the contents of this report.

3.2 WHY IS THERE A LACK OF RESEARCH IN BRITAIN ON PARTICIPATION AND FINANCIAL SUPPORT, COMPARED TO THE UNITED STATES?

Some of the most rigorous research on student participation in further and higher education, and on issues associated with the financial support of students, has been undertaken in the United States. Indeed, there is a long history of conducting such research in the United States. This is in marked contrast to Britain and many other countries. And it is this difference in research agendas that we now explore.

Three main factors help explain the emergence of research on participation and financial support in the United States. First, in the United States most, but not all, students in further and higher education have to pay for their education, especially tuition fees. Education is similar to other consumer goods operating within a market and governed by the economic imperatives of supply and demand. Educational institutions have to attract students to ensure their continued survival. These institutions therefore have a keen interest in understanding the factors affecting student participation and choices. This in turn has helped spur research in the area.

American educational institutions also tend to perceive their students as consumers with all the consumer's associated rights. Their relationship with their students is mediated by the cash nexus. And within this consumer-oriented culture, issues around student satisfaction and completion are high on their agenda. By contrast, British educational institutions are only just beginning to view students in this way. However, because the majority of British students do not meet the full costs of their education, students' role as consumers is not as pronounced as in the United States. Above all in the United States, most educational institutions are attentive to price sensitivity and costs. They are particularly concerned about how changes in the price of education, especially tuition fees, will impact on demand and thus, their enrolments. These concerns have also helped drive the research agenda.

More recently, as competition for students has become more intense, American colleges and universities have responded by developing marketing techniques admissions and financial aid packaging strategies. In particular, educational institutions are increasingly committing their own funds to financial aid packages, to help boost enrolments. As a result, they are concerned about the returns on such investments; the effectiveness of such strategies; whether the amount they invest is sufficient to influence enrolment; and the balance between institutional aid on the one hand, and state and federal aid on the other (Somers, 1995). Although British educational institutions are similarly competing for students, they have adopted very different types of responses. As we saw in Chapter 2, most FE colleges have invested only limited amounts in their hardship funds, unlike American educational institutions.

A second important influence on the development of research on participation in the United Sates is the issue of equality of opportunity, which has been a major concern in the United States, especially since the civil rights movement and other initiatives of the 1960s. Central themes to emerge from this were the underachievement of ethnic groups within the educational system; their lack of equal educational opportunities; and the associated links between educational achievement and poverty (Coleman, 1966). Within this dominant paradigm, education was perceived as a vehicle for social engineering – a key route out of poverty and a major force for achieving equal opportunities. A significant impediment to these goals, however, were the financial barriers in access to further and higher education for low-income and disadvantaged groups. This in turn led to a range of financial aid programmes and policies aimed at boosting the participation of these groups. For instance, the 1965 Higher Education Act instituted a system of loans. It was one of several pieces of radical legislation introduced by the Johnson administration aimed at eliminating poverty and discrimination.

Together, these two dynamics of economics and equal educational opportunities help explain the emergence of a body of literature and research on student participation and the impact of financial support on participation in the United States. These dual forces are also of relevance to the British educational system but they have not been strong enough, to date, to impact seriously on the research agenda.

A third factor which has helped influence the nature of the research undertaken in the United States is the availability of datasources. Unlike Britain, the United States has a wealth of datasets which permit certain types of evaluative research to be conducted. Perhaps most significant are the very well-established longitudinal datasets which allow individuals to be tracked over time, and the time-series datasets which allow changes over time to be charted. These very large datasets are often state funded, are undertaken regularly, and are widely accessible, thus helping shape a particular tradition of research found in the United States, especially in the fields of education and training, and its evaluation.

Consequently, studies in the United States have been able to examine the effects of receiving financial aid on participation and completion or 'enrolment' and 'persistence' – the terms used in the American literature. Moreover they have been able to analyse these issues in robust and sophisticated ways, for instance via econometric modelling. Similarly, these datasets have allowed an exploration of progression which has tended to focus on the transfer of individuals from community colleges to universities.

By contrast, Britain has only two such comparable datasets which are amenable to econometric modelling: the Youth Cohort Survey and the National Child Development Studies. Both have examined issues on participation in post-compulsory education, and where appropriate their findings will be reported in this study. Neither of them, however, have fully explored the issue of financial support and participation nor have they focused specifically on further education.

3.3 WHAT IS THE NATURE OF THE RESEARCH ON PARTICIPATION AND FINANCIAL SUPPORT?

The American research on participation and financial support can be grouped into three categories:

- Econometric analyses of large datasets which model, in various ways, the effects of receiving aid on enrolment and persistence for different types of students.
  These studies have included, for instance, exploration of the impact of financial aid on initial access to further and higher education and on drop-out; evaluation of the effectiveness of different types of financial aid on participation; examination of the impact of changes in tuition fees and grant levels on participation levels; and assessment of the extent to which financial aid reduces the impact of income on educational outcomes in general, and in relation to particular disadvantaged groups.
- Sociological studies which seek to look more broadly at why students leave college, and which locate the influence of financial aid within this broader decision-making context.
- Policy discussions which use the results primarily of the econometric research to assess student financial aid policy.

In Britain, the first and third type of research do not exist. There has been some discussion about policy in Britain but it is largely lacking. First, it is not grounded in, nor informed by, rigorous research. Consequently, much of the debate is based on anecdote and unfounded assertions. Secondly, little consideration has been given to the way in which different policies interact with each other, or to some of the unintended consequences of policies. Finally, discussion has tended to focus on particular policies or policy initiatives rather than a more rounded overview of the funding of FE in its totality.

The second type of sociological research has been undertaken in Britain on a very limited scale. However, there remain large gaps in our knowledge and the research suffers from numerous methodological drawbacks. It is to these issues that we now turn.

3.4 WHAT ARE THE LIMITATIONS OF BRITISH RESEARCH ON PARTICIPATION AND FINANCIAL SUPPORT?

3.4.1 What are the gaps in the research on financial support and participation?

No research has been undertaken which examines the income and expenditure patterns of students in further education. Yet the DfEE regularly funds such research examining this for students in higher education. Indeed, with the introduction of students loans in higher education and the shift in the balance of funding from grants to loans, the Department is obliged to monitor these developments in accordance with the requirements of the 1988 White Paper *Top-up Loans for Students*. The last such study, based on a nationally represent-ative sample of nearly 2,000 full time students (Callender and Kempson, 1996), produced a wealth of information on all the costs associated with participation in higher education and an indication of the extent and nature of student hardship.[16] No such comprehensive information exists for students in further education, so we do not know what exact costs students incur or the exact nature of hardship they may experience.

It is noteworthy that, although issues of access, drop-out and progression in further education have been the subject of some research, many studies have failed to consider the issue of the role of financial support at all. The most stark example of this is work on the Youth Cohort Survey: very limited data on financial support have been collected and analysed while data on individuals' household income are not collected at all in the Survey. In its analysis a derived variable on social class has been used and this could be used as a proxy for household income. However, social class is a very broad measure and it is questionable whether it can be seen as an accurate proxy for the financial circumstances of individual students.

Overall, however, there is a dearth of research on the role of financial support and its effect on initial access to post-compulsory education in general, and to further education in particular. There is even less research which attempts to explore this for different groups of students or which sets out to compare and contrast the position of different types of learners.

No research studies were found which compared the impact of different types of funding or financial support on individuals' decisions to enter further education. In other words, whether for example, discretionary grants are more likely to lead to take-up, compared with a system of training allowances available under Youth Training and some ESF sponsored training in the voluntary sector.

Similarly, none of the literature which was readily available, explored the interplay between financial support and choice of subject or the learning undertaken. Analyses of the Youth Cohort and other research have, however, examined the factors affecting the take-up of academic as against vocational qualifications among 16–18 year olds, and the subjects they chose to study (for example, Payne et al, 1996). Similarly, some research exists which examines differential completion rates by the type of qualification being pursued (Audit Commission/OFSTED, 1993). Yet again, most of these analyses are not explicitly linked to financial support.

Nor are there research studies available on progression and financial support. Data on the destinations of further education students are available from the FEFC but this has not been linked to any data on financial support.

Gaps in the available research and literature have inevitably put constraints upon the scope of this literature review and impacted upon this study.

3.4.2 What are the methodological limitations of the research on financial support and participation?

The few studies which have explored the issue of financial support and initial access or completion have been very small-scale. They are often based on the experiences of one particular college and a small number of students.

None of these studies are based on nationally representative samples of colleges or students. Yet, as we have seen in Chapter 2, there are considerable regional variations in policies concerning financial support and also in the costs of living. In addition, the composition of the student body in terms of class and age varies from one college to another depending on its locality, and drop-out rates vary considerably. As a result, the conclusions which can be drawn from these studies are very limited. It would be very misleading to

---

16 The study did not, however, include the growing numbers of part-time students in higher education whose financial position is likely to be very different from full-timers. This is primarily because part-time students are not eligible for either mandatory awards or student loans – the main source of state-funded student support in higher education.

assume that what pertains to one college applies to all colleges and to all students across the country as a whole.

The existing research shows that a combination of factors are likely to influence an individual's decision to enter FE, drop out or progress. In the absence of large datasets or large sample sizes it is, however, very difficult to isolate the impact of financial support – be it positive or negative – from this wide range of contributory factors. Certain analytical techniques are available which can help isolate the impact of a single factor. But they are rarely used, primarily, but not exclusively, because the sample sizes are too small.

Indeed overall, the analytical tools used in most existing studies are very simplistic, unlike those used in American studies. So too is the overall approach to the research; often it is just not rigorous or methodologically robust. This is not to dismiss the research which has been undertaken. It does fulfil a role. However, if it is usefully to inform policy development, it must be based on sound methods which produce reliable results.

The methodological simplicity of research in this area can be readily illustrated in relation to studies on drop-out. First, there is often no clear definition of what is meant by the term drop-out or non-completion and thus which students fall within the remit of the study. For instance, non-completers could be students who:

- drop out of their course entirely and leave education;
- stop taking one course and change to another course or qualification;
- continue taking units from one course and do or do not participate in another course;
- complete a course but do not pass the final examination;
- take more time to undertake a course than usually designated for the course.

Indeed, a major problem in assessing completion and non-completion rates is the variety of terms and definitions used by different institutions, bodies, and studies. The term 'drop-out' tends to be widely used to describe any form of withdrawal before the course's completion date, but of course some qualifications (for example, NVQs) are not formally time bound. Other terms include wastage, exits, attrition, withdrawal, non-persistence, non-completion, non-continuation. These terms can be and often are, defined in different ways or not defined at all. This makes it difficult to compare official statistics and institutional studies (McGivney, 1996).

The second major limitation of research on drop-out is that, with a few recent exceptions (for example, Medway and Penney, 1994; CSET, 1994), studies do not include a control group of students who have not dropped out against which to compare those who have dropped out. This problem also occurs in studies on participation. In other words, the studies concentrate solely on those who drop out. Such an approach implicitly assumes that drop-outs are a distinctive group with very different characteristics and in different situations from completers. Yet, it is not known if this is the case. Nor is it possible with such an approach to isolate the factors which are particular to those dropping out. A focus on early leavers may conceal continuities of attitudes and experience which extend to students who have not withdrawn.

A third drawback with existing studies on drop-out is that they are often based on information gathered from staff or inspectors (for example, Audit Commission/OFSTED, 1993) and not from students (for example, HMI, 1991). Yet staff may have very different perspectives on why students leave compared with the students themselves. Moreover, different types of staff are likely to have different views depending on the nature of their contact with students and their position in the institution. These issues have not been considered properly in the majority of existing studies.

Studies which rely exclusively on data on student withdrawals collected by colleges are also open to question. Colleges tend to use the data collection system recommended in 1987 by DES/WO. This involves a member of the teaching staff completing a return and attributing the reason for withdrawal to one of a number of predetermined factors, usually after four weeks of non-attendance by the student.

This approach is flawed for a number of reasons. First, it requires the member of staff to choose 'one main reason', which precludes any analysis of multiple causality. Second, the system places the onus for data collection on the teacher which may make it difficult to collect accurate information, either because the withdrawing student may be reluctant to communicate any implied or direct criticism of the course, or because the teacher may be reluctant to listen to such criticism. These issues have implications for the reliability of data collected by the FEFC on Individual Student Records.

In addition, even where students are included in the studies, the research is sometimes designed so that students are only allowed to identify one factor which led to their withdrawal. Furthermore, the research rarely examines the issue of participation from the combined perspective of staff and students. In other words, any differences between the views of these two groups are not explored – yet the discontinuities could help inform more rounded initiatives to reduce withdrawal.

Finally, studies on all aspects of participation – not just drop-out – only rarely tackle, tease out or acknowledge the complexities of the decision-making process and the role played by financial issues. Few qualitative studies have been conducted which explore in-depth why people decide to enter, drop out, or progress and how these decisions interact with financial decisions. An individual's financial circumstances are often perceived as 'socially acceptable' reasons for non-participation or dropping out. Yet, it is well established that financial reasons can be a post-hoc rationalisation for non-participation and mask other issues in a wide variety of activities, not just in education.

Studies using quantitative methods do not allow a full exploration of these decision-making issues. Nor do they permit, unlike qualitative studies, a full understanding of financial hardship and what dynamics of participation may lead to financial hardship. In fact, these issues are often ignored in quantitative studies. Financial hardship or problems are not defined in the studies. Objective measures of hardship are rarely used, for instance, where students do identify financial hardship this is not assessed against their income and expenditure.

These are some of the reasons why existing research is so lacking and why new research is urgently required.

3.5 SUMMARY

Unlike the United States, there is no history in Britain of conducting research on the relationship between participation and student support in further or higher education. Consequently, there is a dearth of such studies in Britain. Key British studies which have examined the issues of initial access to FE, drop-out, and progression have mostly failed to explore the impact of financial support on these issues. They have tended to be preoccupied with the impact of social class rather than focusing on either income or financial aid.

The gaps in research are particularly pronounced in relation to studies on the actual costs of participation and on the role of student support on initial access and in particular progression.

The few studies which have been conducted are limited both in their scale and in the methods used. As a result, it is very difficult to generalise from these studies or to give an accurate assessment of the impact of financial support on participation. However, if research is usefully to inform policy development, it must be based on sound methods which produce reliable results.

Chapter 4

Financial support and access

4.1 INTRODUCTION

The purpose of this chapter is to examine the relationship between financial support, or the lack of it, and access to further education and training. It begins with a brief overview of current participation and non-participation levels in the sector and the changes over time. Then, by way of setting the discussion in context, it briefly examines the non-financial factors which affect access. Finally, it assesses the ways in which financial support can act as an incentive and conversely, how the lack of support works as a disincentive.

4.2 WHAT ARE THE PARTICIPATION AND NON-PARTICIPATION LEVELS?[17]

4.2.1 How has participation changed?

The further education sector has experienced substantial growth over the past few years. For example, between 1982 and 1992 the number of students enrolled in the sector increased from 1.3 million to approximately 2 million (DfEE, 1993). By 1995/1996 some 3.5 million students were enrolled in colleges of further education in England alone, an increase of 17 per cent from the previous year (FEFC, 1996b). Indeed, some of this growth has been fuelled by government policy.

Participation among 16–19 year olds, particularly in full-time education, has been rising since 1986. In 1986/87 approximately 50 per cent of 16 year olds were enrolled in full-time education; by 1994/95 this had increased to 70 per cent. By 1995/96 approximately 727,300 under 19 year olds had enrolled in further education sector colleges in England (FEFC, 1996b), an increase of nearly 2 per cent on the previous year. However, there are signs that the rate of growth among younger students has been slowing since 1991.

Adult participation has also followed an upward trend, but the increases have been much more marked compared to under 19 year olds. For example, between 1985 and 1993 the number of adults participating in the sector had increased from approximately 900,000 to over 1.5 million (Steedman and Green, 1996). By 1995/96, there were nearly 2.5 million 19–59 year olds enrolled in further education sector colleges, an increase of over a quarter on the previous year (FEFC, 1996b).

---

17 For a fuller discussion of participation, see Steedman and Green, 1996.

4.2.2   What are the patterns of participation?

However, the patterns of participation for the different age groups vary considerably. The latest statistics show that nearly four out of five students (79 per cent) on FEFC funded provision are adults and the remainder are under the age of 19. 'Traditional' 16–18 year olds now constitute one in five of the students in Council-funded provision and this trend is set to continue. Moreover, while the majority of adult students (90 per cent) are studying part-time, most under 19-year-old students are full-time (72 per cent) (FEFC, 1996b).

4.2.3   Which groups are under-represented in further education?

Despite these overall increases, there are still a number of groups who are under-represented in further education and training. For example, NIACE survey findings confirm those of other British research in revealing a continuing under-representation of people in lower socio-economic categories in various forms of post-school education and training. Although there have been some advances, particularly by women and ethnic minority adults, the groups of non-participants remain largely the same as those identified by researchers such as McGivney in 1990. And even then, she noted that these groups had not changed substantially from previous years (McGivney, 1990). The groups, many of which overlap, include:

- unskilled manual workers
- people without qualifications
- unemployed people
- some groups of women (those in the lower socio-economic groups and lone parents
- some ethnic minority groups (for example, refugees)
- older adults (50 plus)
- people with special needs and disabilities
- people with literacy and/or numeracy difficulties
- ex-offenders.

To this list can be added the growing number of part-time and temporary workers largely excluded from employer-provided training.

Not all these groups are totally excluded from further education and training, but they do experience varying degrees of difficulty in gaining access and achieving successful outcomes. In addition, the situation for some groups has worsened over the years, while for others there has been little advance (Uden, 1994). For example, a comparison of MORI poll findings in 1994 with a similar poll in 1990 revealed that the number of older people benefiting from education and training has declined at a time when they are a growing proportion of the population (Sargant, 1991; NIACE, 1994).

Detailed information on the extent to which all these groups are under-represented in further education is not readily available. For instance, comprehensive data on students with disabilities who are in further education are not easily obtainable although some information is collected by the FEFC. A recent survey estimated that in 1995 in further education colleges in England there were about 126,500 students with learning difficulties and/or a disability (FEFC, 1997). However, it is not possible to assess the potential pool of students with disabilities in the population at large, against which to measure the extent of under-representation (FEFC, 1997).

In addition, certain types of under-represented groups appear to have particular problems gaining access to certain types of training. For instance, there are an estimated 6 million adults who experience some difficulty with writing and numeracy. Yet, this group is under-represented on government schemes. In 1993, people with literacy and numeracy needs accounted for only 8 per cent of those starting Training for Work. Moreover, of those who do gain access to these schemes, only 30 per cent achieve a qualification, compared with the average of 40 per cent overall (Meager and Wiliams, 1994, in Uden, 1994).

By contrast, some groups are over-represented on certain types of training, in part because of their limited access to different forms of education and training provision. For instance, ethnic minorities are often over-represented on government training schemes. However, among this group the key issue is not access but outcomes. A higher proportion of black and Asian people stay on in post compulsory education than white people, but they are less likely than white people to gain a job or qualification at the end (Uden, 1994).

4.3 WHAT NON-FINANCIAL FACTORS AFFECT ACCESS TO FURTHER EDUCATION AND TRAINING?

This section will give a very brief overview of some of the key non-financial factors affecting participation in further education.[18] The reasons for participation and non-participation are numerous, complex and much debated (McGivney, 1990). They can be broadly divided into structural, institutional, dispositional and situational factors. Together these factors limit opportunities for participation and inhibit individuals from taking advantage of the opportunities available.

4.3.1 Which structural factors affect participation?

Academic ability and social class have been singled out as the strongest determinants of educational participation and attainment among research studies on access to and opportunities in education, both in Britain and the United States. They have been particularly important in explaining and predicting patterns of post-compulsory education among 16–18 year olds.

For instance, analyses of the Youth Cohort Study have consistently found that young people's prior educational experience and, in particular, their O level and GCSE examination results have a strong impact on their participation levels. As increasing proportions of young people obtain GCSE passes, the proportion participating in post-compulsory education has similarly increased (Gray et al, 1993; Payne et al, 1996).

It is also well established that educational achievement is associated with social class. Recent analyses of the Youth Cohort Survey suggest that parental occupation has a powerful effect on the likelihood of staying on at all levels of GSCE results. In 1993, 85 per cent of children of non-manual parents stayed on, compared to 65 per cent of children of manual workers (Payne et al, 1996, p102). Among young people with good GSCE results, differences by parental occupation have narrowed. By contrast, for those with poorer results, differences by social class have widened. The reason is that although staying-on rates have increased in all groups, they increased more slowly for young people from low-skilled backgrounds (Payne et al, 1996). These trends exist even when individuals' sex, region and ethnic group are taken into account.

Employment status and the state of the labour market are further significant determinants of access to further education and training. Employment is an increasingly important source of further education but those outside the labour market, or on the periphery, are excluded from such provision. However, it is well established that training opportunities among the employed are not equally distributed. Those higher up the occupational hierarchy have the greatest access along with those working in large establishments (Rigg, 1989; Gallie and White, 1993).

---

18 For a fuller discussion of these issues, see Steedman and Green, 1996.

The state of the labour market also influences access to education and training. For employed adults, education and training opportunities tend to decline during times of recession. In contrast, for 16–18 year olds, there is some evidence to suggest that participation in post-compulsory education rises when the youth labour market is tight. However, as Steedman and Green (1996, para 2.4.1) comment 'the research to date has provided little conclusive evidence of the precise relationships between the two'.

Policy initiatives can impact both positively and negatively on participation rates. For instance, to date, incorporation has contributed to a growth in participation but the current Treasury allocations to the sector may lead to a reduction in provision. The Further and Higher Education Act (1992) has had a variable effect on students with disabilities. Older students and those with severe disabilities have been disadvantaged with the drive for certification, while for those who can overcome that hurdle, funding has become more secure. Indeed, colleges have reported a 57 per cent increase in enrolment of students with disabilities (Uden, 1994).

4.3.2 Which institutional factors affect participation?

The education system itself may influence the take-up of education and training.

Cultural values of educational institutions have also been singled out as influencing participation. Some have argued that certain sections of the community, such as the working classes and ethnic minorities, do not readily participate in further education and training partly because they perceive the system to be part of the culture pattern of certain ethnic and socio-economic groups, that is the white middle classes. In other words, they find the cultural values of the education system alienating.

Institutional and organisational structures can also inhibit participation. These include factors such as:

- entry requirements
- recruitment methods and practices
- location of the provision
- type of courses
- structure of the course
- timing of courses
- course contents.

McGivney (1996) suggests that the recent expansion in adult participation in further education has been encouraged by increasing flexibility in entry requirements, course structures, learning modes and assessment methods.

The qualification system and the contents of the qualifications, both academic and vocational, have also been widely criticised for depressing participation rates. In particular, the complexity and fragmented nature of the system hves been highlighted. In turn, this means it is difficult for individuals to understand what qualifications and courses are available, and most suited to their needs.

Access to information can, therefore, also influence the take-up of education and training. Indeed, a review of research into disadvantaged adult groups estimated that up to two-thirds of non-participants simply did not know what learning opportunities existed (Osborn et al, 1980). Other research shows how the absence of information may limit individuals' choices. For instance, early research on NVQs found that the lack of knowledge was a major barrier to take-up among individuals (McHugh et al, 1993). More recent research (Callender, 1997b) suggests this is no longer a significant obstacle although a lack of understanding may be. However, as Hedoux (1981) has shown, even where people knew about educational opportunities and were favourably disposed to them, they still failed to participate. Knowledge and understanding may be essential but not sufficient prerequisites to enrolment.

4.3.3 Which dispositional factors affect participation?

The attitudes, perceptions and expectations of people towards further education have been shown to play a significant role in non-participation (McGivney, 1990). These include:

- the inappropriateness and lack of relevance of further education;
- a lack of awareness of learning needs;
- individuals' belief that they are too old to learn;
- individuals' lack of confidence in their ability to learn.

In Britain, there is very little doubt that a large proportion of the adult population considers education totally irrelevant. In a recent survey of non-participation, 60 per cent of non-participants claimed to have no interest whatsoever in adult education and many expressed strong hostility to education in general.

4.3.4 Which situational factors affect participation?

Lack of time is a barrier to participation which is often cited by adults in both American and British surveys. This constraint arises primarily out of domestic responsibilities and work schedules, with those employed part-time or doing shift work reporting the most difficulties. However, people without job-related obligations are less likely to take up further education and training. Therefore, an increase in leisure time does not necessarily lead to an increase in the take-up of training. Indeed, a time-budget study in the US showed that a general increase in leisure hours was almost entirely absorbed by an increase in television watching, for non-educational purposes (McGivney, 1990).

Family responsibilities are one contributory factor especially to women's lack of time to participate in further education. These responsibilities may also inhibit participation, particularly when combined with inadequate transport and lack of childcare provision (Maguire et al, 1993). These are just some of the factors impacting on women's participation.

Finally, the cost of further education and training and the availability of financial support can influence access – the rest of the chapter looks at this in more detail.

4.4 DOES FINANCIAL SUPPORT ACT AS AN INCENTIVE?

4.4.1 What is the evidence from British studies?

There is limited research in Britain which shows that financial support acts as an incentive to initial access to further education. In particular, training allowances and fee remission policies have been shown to have a positive effect, as have Career Development Loans.

As already discussed in Chapter 2, training allowances are given to young people participating in Youth Training. A recent review of the programme by the DfEE concluded that the low level of training allowance paid to young people is considered a 'significant factor in the decision of a few young people to refuse training or leave early'. The research recommended that the effects of different allowance rates on participation and training providers' funding should be examined (DfEE, 1996a).

Other research confirms that unemployed people are more likely to be attracted to training which offers allowances. The evidence suggests that training allowances which are paid independently of social security benefits have a more positive effect on people's motivation than top-ups to benefit. As a tutor for the unemployed in McGivney's (1992) study pointed out:

> There is an important psychological benefit to having the training allowance rather than benefit. A training allowance gives people a different relationship to the world. Employment Training is just a continuation of benefit and people may not come just because of that.

An earlier study by McGivney (1990) on access to education among non-participant adults, revealed similar findings in relation to fee concessions. Where an LEA with no fee concessionary policy introduced a voucher scheme whereby people on benefit could purchase a voucher which entitled them to join as many classes as they wished for one term, there was an overwhelming response. Moreover, 40 per cent were first-time participants. The unemployed were also attracted to the scheme because the enrolment procedures were non-threatening and the vouchers freed them from the stigma of regularly producing proof of benefit in order to be given a concession.[19]

Similarly, in the same study, McGivney (1990) showed that in a rural area concessionary fees had been instrumental in attracting a number of non-participant groups. Indeed, 60 per cent of the enrollees at the centre were in concessionary fee categories and some people spent the entire day there because it was cheaper than being at home.

The introduction of fee remission policy at Richmond Adult and Community College also had a similar effect. Fee remission allowed unemployed students to enrol on a number of part-time courses; a high proportion of the new students were people who had left school at the earliest opportunity (NIACE REPLAN, 1988, in McGivney,1992).

There is some evidence to suggest that Career Development Loans, discussed in Chapter 2, have acted as a financial incentive and a motivating factor. For example, in 1995/96, 84 per cent of CDL trainees reported that they would not have trained, in the absence of loans. This figure has actually increased over the years from 77 per cent in 1991/93 (DfEE, 1996f). However, as we have seen, the take-up of these loans is limited and not as great as originally envisaged when they were introduced. And as will be seen from the American literature, loans have been shown to disadvantage low-income students and are not as powerful an incentive in comparison to grants or allowances.

4.4.2   What is the evidence from American studies?

As discussed in the previous chapter, there is an extensive body of American literature on the impact of student support on participation in further and higher education. However, it is important to remember when examining the findings from this research that both the impetus behind it, and the educational context, are very different when compared to Britain.

Numerous national studies conducted in the United States have examined the enrolment behaviour of school leavers – high school students. These studies are primarily concerned with access to higher education which includes community colleges – which are the nearest equivalent that the American education system has to FE colleges in Britain.

The studies, using a variety of econometric techniques, show unequivocally that financial support has a positive impact on student enrolment, especially among students from low-income families. For example, a study of how financial aid affected the decisions of high school seniors to attend college in 1972, 1980, and 1982 demonstrated that all types of financial aid facilitated college attendance for all groups of students, and especially those from low-income families (St John and Noell, 1989). Studies have tested different types of models for assessing the impact of financial aid. For instance, Somers and St John (1993)

---

19   Since incorporation, the FEFC has adopted a standardised policy on fee remission. Before 1992, fee remission policies were decided by each LEA.

tested a model for assessing the impact of aid offers on 2,558 accepted students' college enrolment decisions. The analysis revealed that financial aid strategies have a substantial influence on enrolment. In addition, the systematic analysis of student enrolment decisions can help institutional administrators refine their financing decisions.

Much research in the United States has been concerned with the net price of higher education, namely, the impact of tuition fees on first-time enrolments. These studies generally have shown that increases in tuition costs depress enrolment levels among students from low income groups but not those from high-income groups (McPherson and Shapiro, 1991; Leslie and Brinkman, 1988; McPherson, 1978).

Leslie and Brinkman (1987) reviewed and undertook a meta-analysis of 25 studies concerning the relationship between tuition charges and enrolment. They showed a remarkable consistency in these studies' results, despite the fact that the studies were all very different. All twenty-five of the studies confirmed that enrolment declined when prices were raised and increased when prices were lowered. The modal result was that for every $100 increase in tuition fees, the participation rate for 18–24 year olds fell by 0.6 per cent and enrolment declined by 1.8 per cent, *ceteris paribus.*

Leslie and Brinkman's (1987) review included research examining the behaviour of students from all social classes, not just those from low-income families. They concluded that where these studies considered broader issues other than just the economic effects on enrolment rates, that 'sociological variables invariably have turned out to be [the] most prominent; economic variables rank about third. In other words, college attendance is associated more with such student traits as social class and parent's education than with college price' (Leslie and Brinkman (1987, p195). However, they also caution that it cannot be assumed that all price changes impact on enrolments equally. Inevitably for some type of students, such as low-income students, student support has a greater impact and may rank higher in determining enrolment.

More recent research has been concerned to specify separately the impact on enrolments of changes both in tuition fees and the American equivalent to maintenance grants and to loans. It has adopted a differentiated-price approach (St John and Starkey, 1995). This research has shown how students do not necessarily respond to grant awards and/or loans in the same way that they respond to tuition charges (McPherson and Shapiro, 1991; St John, 1990, 1991). Students respond to a set of prices rather than a single price, and students with different levels of need respond differently to tuition and student aid.

The emerging consensus in this research is that financial aid packages which include monies for both tuition and maintenance do have a positive impact on enrolment. And the amount of grants awarded has more influence on enrolment decisions by low-income students than tuition charges (St John, 1990). Most research also indicates that grants were a more effective tool than loans or other forms of student aid in encouraging enrolment, especially for the lowest income groups and minority groups (St John and Noell, 1989; St John, 1990). However, middle-income students are more favourably influenced by loans.

Other research has focused on the spending patterns of different states on student financial aid rather than concentrating on the individual. It examines how state policies regarding the setting of tuition rates and financial aid budgets affect access to public higher education. It also confirms that at least among some groups, higher levels of grant spending are associated with higher enrolment rates (Heller, 1996).

4.5   DOES THE LACK OF FINANCIAL SUPPORT ACT AS A DISINCENTIVE?

4.5.1   What is the evidence from British studies?

Just as the availability of financial support has been shown to be a positive incentive to initial access to further education and training, conversely, the lack of it is often cited as a disincentive. For example, a survey to establish baselines for National Targets for Education and Training indicated that lack of finance was the most common barrier to learning. This was highlighted by 42 per cent of the 1,200 adult respondents (Boullen, 1996).

Are all groups equally affected by financial barriers?

The relative importance of financial barriers tends to vary with different groups. According to the research, those mostly likely to be affected are: adults; unemployed people; and women. For example, Hunt and Jackson (1992) identify the current financial support system as one of six factors inhibiting wider participation among adult learners. McGivney's (1990) survey of non-participants showed that funding was clearly a barrier for the unemployed and certain groups of women. By contrast, other groups, such as the unskilled/semi-skilled workers, older adults and ethnic minorities, were deterred more by factors related to personal circumstances, family, work, and patterns of living. Similarly, Maguire et al (1993; 1996) in their literature review of the factors influencing individuals' commitment to lifelong learning also point to funding as a particular barrier to participation.

What type of financial barriers do individuals experience?

Some of the most widely cited financial barriers to participation include tuition fees, the add-on costs of training, and other indirect costs such as childcare. Other costs associated with participation have been discussed in Chapter 2 (Section 2.2) and will not be repeated here. All of them, however, can be a potential obstacle to participation.

Inevitably, which costs act as a barrier is likely to vary depending on the group. For example, for those who are entitled to fee remission, fees would not be an issue while for mothers of young children, childcare costs may be an inhibiting factor. As De Bell (1993) has asserted, the nature of financial costs associated with training are such that they can escalate simply due to the nature of travel or childcare costs. Potential applicants are, however, unlikely to say if this is the case. They simply do not enrol.

Mansell's (1997) work has stressed the issue of rising transport costs both in urban and rural areas for both young and older students. He suggests that this problem may be hidden but is potentially impacting on participation. He cites an example of this in the way one college's student population has changed because of the lack of transport subsidies. The college used to recruit from across the country, but with the ending of travel subsidies, it has reduced its catchment area.

What these particular findings suggest is that a relatively small cost can potentially act as a deterrent. In other words, marginal costs, which may seem insignificant, can make the difference between participation and non-participation (De Bell, 1993). In turn, this has implications for policy development. It is possible that relatively small grants could widen participation considerably. However, until more extensive research is undertaken which systematically analyses the scale of financial hardship and its nature, such a conclusion can only be very tentative.

However, other research about the deterrent effects of tuition fees contradicts such a conclusion. Fees, unlike travel expenses, are a major cost. Both an NIAE (1970) and ACACE (1982) report described how increased participation in adult education by people from lower socio-economic groups was abruptly reversed as a result of frequent and steep fee increases in the second half of the 1980s. Local surveys confirmed this development (Daines et al, 1982; ALFA, 1987).

McGivney (1990) in her review on the subject of the deterrent effect on fees (and other costs) concluded that while there is no doubt that increased fee levels affect the most economically disadvantaged, the evidence overall is inconclusive and contradictory.

What are individuals' perceptions of the costs?

In spite of the fact that cost is often cited as a major barrier to access, research has shown that non-participants usually have little idea of the *actual* cost of participating in further education and training. Many non-participants automatically expect costs to be beyond their reach. This is often compounded by their lack of knowledge of the funding options available to them. This has led some researchers to believe that cost, like time, has become a socially acceptable reason for not participating, possibly masking more complex reasons (McGivney, 1990; Wirral Metropolitan College, 1993; De Bell, 1993).

However, the results of the recent Wirral Metropolitan College (1993) survey in which prospective and actual students were required to complete comparable questionnaires, showed the perceived financial barriers matched closely with those actually experienced by students. The perceived and actual costs causing difficulty included travel costs, childcare costs, college fees, the cost of books and equipment and the loss of income. The only costs not identified by potential students, but incurred by actual students, related to unexpected expenses such as moving home (Wirral Metropolitan College, 1993).

Any mismatch between perceived and actual costs raises questions about the availability of information on the nature and level of financial costs of participation. The only student services that colleges are required to provide are FEFC stipulated recruitment guidance and support (Page, 1996). Though many provide services beyond the minimum, overall the extent and nature of provision appear to vary widely.

In addition to availability, and perhaps more important, is the issue of access to information on costs and funding sources. Prospective students who have ready access to this type of information would be better placed to make an informed decision, than those who do not. Similarly, as indicated in Chapter 2, differing capacities to access funding to cover the costs of training could also influence the decision of whether or not to participate. Yet no research has been undertaken that systematically examines the impact of access to information about financial support on participation.

4.5.2   What is the evidence from American studies?

The relative importance of finance as a barrier also varies across countries. A comparison of stated deterrents in Britain and the United States revealed that the costs of participation were of less importance in the American sample, but considered a significant deterrent by the British respondents. This possibly reflects, among other things, the income gap between the two countries (Darkenwald, 1988 in McGivney, 1990).

Yet there is evidence from studies conducted in the United States that the lack of financial support has acted as a disincentive. Much of the literature has focused on two twin developments: the changes in policies on financial aid to college students and the decline in college attendance among African-American students by the late 1980s. Hauser and Anderson (1991) showed how between 1975 and the mid-1980s fewer African-American high school seniors were planning to attend college compared to Whites.

What has been the impact of student loans on participation?

During the 1970s financial aid in the United States was increasingly offered to middle-income groups. Furthermore, there was a shift to the increasing use of repayable loans. Increasing evidence suggested that low-income students were less willing to take out loans because they were concerned that their lifetime earnings from a college education would not repay the costs incurred from loan indebtedness (College Entrance Examination Board, 1983; 1990; Mortenson, 1990). Loans therefore often discouraged or prohibited low-income students from participating in higher education. As Mortenson in his study of the impact of increased loan utilisation by low-income students commented:

> Higher education is a far riskier investment decision for low-income students because they characteristically demonstrate less promise for academic success, and hence are less likely to earn the higher incomes following graduation that enable them to repay their loan obligation. (1990, pi)

The pre-college family income of college students is strongly correlated with the eventual success of students in college (Mumper and Vander Ark, 1991). As a result, low-income students are less likely to finish college, and those who finish are less likely to do well. This higher risk of failure serves to discourage disadvantaged students from borrowing the large sums necessary to enrol in higher education.

Despite the introduction of student loans in Britain in the early 1990s, no equivalent research has been undertaken which examines the impact of loans on initial access to higher education in the UK. Rather research has focused on the take-up of loans among *existing* undergraduate students. For example, Callender and Kempson (1996) found that a third of students who were eligible for a loan had never taken one out. Payne and Callender's (1997) further analysis showed that a key reason why students did not take out a loan was concern about debt and a dislike of borrowing. Moreover, they demonstrated that students from lower social classes were more likely to take out a loan than those from higher social classes. In addition, these low-income students tended to take out the largest loans and thus incur the highest debts. Although the conditions attached to the repayment of students loans are different in Britain compared with the United States, the more widespread use of loans in Britain may well have a negative impact on participation especially among low-income students.

What has been the impact of cuts in student grants on participation?

During the 1980s there were further cuts in federal aid to students in the United States. In particular, grants aimed at needy students were greatly weakened when the Reagan administration did not increase aid to meet the rising costs of higher education and the effects of inflation (Baker and Velez, 1996).

Research has demonstrated that these decreases in the amount and form of financial aid have particularly affected potential students from low-income families (Orfield, 1992). Moreover, they have been identified as the strongest factor contributing to the decline in African American school leavers attending college (Hauser, 1992; Clotfelter, 1993). Using Mortenson's (1990) analysis, Hauser (1992) concluded that African-Americans were less willing to borrow for higher education for both economic and psychological reasons. He commented that 'a student's willingness to borrow will be affected by the economic return to his or her investment' (pp302–3) and given that many of these students come from low-income families 'a typical $10–12,000 debt will often be larger than his or her families income' (p304).

The American experience suggests that the proposed abolition of student grants in Britain may well have a depressing effect on the enrolment among certain groups of potential higher education students in Britain. Whatever the changes introduced, they will need to be carefully monitored to assess their impact on the composition of the student body.

4.6 HOW DOES THE LACK OF FINANCIAL SUPPORT AFFECT PARTICULAR GROUPS OF STUDENTS?

4.6.1 How does the lack of financial support affect mature and younger students?

Finance as a barrier to access may be of greater significance to mature as opposed to younger students. As Bryant and Noble (1989) have pointed out, mature and second chance students tend to come from lower socio-economic backgrounds and, as mentioned in Chapter 2, they have more limited funding options open to them.

Drawing on their survey of mature students on a particular course at Ruskin College between 1981 and 1986, Bryant and Noble (1989) found that questions of finance and grant problems deterred candidates from even applying for the course. They contend that, each year, once prospective students were informed of the level of grant awards, some still did not apply. This was because the prospective students believed that the financial risks and sacrifices were too great. Married women with family and housing commitments were most likely to be deterred at this stage. Further, some students applied and secured a place but did not take it up due to financial reasons. The authors estimate that this affected about 10 per cent of students who were offered places.

This study's results clearly indicate that it is not only the *availability* of financial support which influences the decision of prospective students to take up further education and training, but also the *amount* of support. These findings echo those from American studies, discussed above.

Other research conducted in the 1970s and 80s confirms that the lack of finance may have had a negative impact on the wider participation among adults from lower socio-economic groups (NIAE, 1970; ACACE, 1982). And local surveys support this. For instance, Daines' et al (1982) survey in south-east Derbyshire showed that sharp fee increases resulted in a 28 per cent fall in enrolments among those with relatively less disposable income. A survey in Newcastle-upon-Tyne (ALFA, 1987) showed that a 65 per cent increase in LEA fees between 1979 and 1983 led to a 22 per cent fall in enrolment, particularly in poor neighbourhoods.

McGivney (1990) suggests that while there is little doubt that increased fees would affect the participation of economically disadvantaged groups, the evidence overall is contradictory and inconclusive. In her research on adult non-participation in the late 1980s, fewer than nine per cent of respondents cited cost as a deterrent to participation. Moreover, information gathered from LEA providers suggested that cost may be less of a barrier than generally supposed, although certain groups such as elderly and unemployed people do require some financial concessions and assistance.

De Bell and Davies (1991) in their survey of the Norfolk and Waveney area also highlighted the plight of prospective adult students. The results of their study indicated that though many people were prepared to fund their own training and had the commitment and motivation to participate, they were barred from doing so due to financial reasons. De Bell and Davies (1991) identified five adult groups who were particularly likely to encounter financial barriers. These included:

- young adults (19–25) with skills deficits attempting to undertake training after a period of time out of formal education;

- unemployed and recently redundant adults, including older unemployed adults (45+)
- women working at home and seeking training for return to paid employment;
- employed adults seeking training to enhance employability or earnings potential where they are not supported by their employers;
- adults with special training needs.

Each group will now be examined, with the exception of the employed and unemployed, where discussion has been reserved for the next section (4.6.2).

What is the impact on young adults?

De Bell and Davies' (1991) research showed that the circumstances of young adults were different from other adults in several ways. Young adults tended to experience a lack of financial support where they are in low-paid, low-skilled jobs, or were unqualified. For those young adults who were still living at home and beginning to acquire financial independence, participation in training often involved a loss or reduction in income which could impact negatively on their whole family. For young adults who had had children comparatively early and therefore did not have the qualifications needed to secure work at income levels to support their families, returning to training was seen as an investment in their future. However, they tended to encounter financial barriers. In some instances, family income from work was too low to accommodate the costs of training. For those in receipt of social security benefit, getting a discretionary grant did not necessarily lead to additional income because the two systems tended to cancel each other out. Childcare costs were also a major barrier and these were compounded where there was more than one child (De Bell and Davies, 1991).

What is the impact on women and women returners?

Women, in De Bell and Davies' (1991) study (43 per cent of the respondents), experienced particular financial problems. Like all families with young children, the cost of childcare was a major barrier to women in general, and women returners, in particular. Childcare costs debarred women from undertaking training even when provision was available.

In addition, women were reluctant to enrol in training if it jeopardised the family budget. Women tended to place family need, particularly their children's care above personal aspiration. This was even the case where the only alternative was low-paid, part-time work which failed to use their skills, qualifications, and experience (De Bell and Davies, 1991). In many instances, women in such jobs did not have access to money to pay for training which would have led to a better paying job. And rarely do these types of jobs offer training opportunities sponsored by the womens' employers (Callender and Metcalf, 1997).[20] Some experienced resistance from their partners to spending money on their own training while others did not feel that they had the right to use family money on themselves. As De Bell (1992, p9) pointed out 'again and again the research team found that women placed family and children above their own training needs in managing family budgets'. This is confirmed by other research which showed that unemployed women were unwilling to use family income to enrol in training (Callender, 1987).

What is the impact on adults with special training needs?

Adults with special training needs also face financial barriers. A recent survey of FE provision in England for students with learning difficulties and/or a disability (FEFC, 1997) confirmed this. The vast majority of colleges surveyed, with systems for recording unmet

---

20 For a much more detailed examination of women and training see Callender and Metcalf, 1997.

need, reported that they had had to turn away students with disabilities because they were unable to meet their specific needs. Consequently, some students with disabilities would have been barred from training as they could not afford to personally pay for the services they needed.

According to De Bell and Davies (1991), a further financial barrier to adults with special educational needs arose from the local council's charges on basic adult educational services. For these adults, Basic Skills training was necessary before they could fully participate in work-related training and the fees for adult educational services may inhibit this process.

What is the impact on older adults?

The number of older people benefiting from further education has declined in recent years. This can be largely attributed to two factors. First, one of the effects of the Further and Higher Education Act (1992) has been a shift from uncertificated to certificated courses by providers. This shift, in part, is a result of changes in how colleges are funded. Second, the reduction in local authority funding has hit LEA education for adults particularly hard. Most older people have little interest in gaining qualifications and they are unwilling and cannot afford to travel long distances when local classes are withdrawn. Moreover, many find the increasing cost of learning (especially outside the FEFC umbrella) a formidable barrier (Uden, 1994).

4.6.2 How does the lack of financial support affect unemployed and employed students?

A key feature of recent government policy on education and training is its non-interventionist approach. This sees employers rather than the state as having the key role in providing training. It encourages employers to shape the contents of training, and increasingly education, so that it meets their needs. It relies upon the market to meet training needs and upon individuals to pursue their own careers and take responsibility for their training and education needs. As a recent Employment Minister, James Paice, is quoted to have said:

> People are at the heart of our competitiveness and future prosperity, but for too long many have seen education and training as something that just happens to them. That attitude needs to change. People are responsible for their own futures. (Littlefield, 1995)

While the Minister recognised the role of employers he said that responsibility 'rests ultimately with the individual'. However, the government does have a role in providing and supporting education and training for those with no access to employers' training, namely, the unemployed and those outside the labour market, such as women returners.

What is the impact on unemployed people?

The lack of personal funds as well as the inadequacy of the benefit system to fund training are particular problems for the unemployed. As discussed in Chapter 2, there are very real difficulties surrounding the funding of unemployed people who participate in further education and training. Indeed, in McGivney's report on motivating unemployed adults to undertake education and training, she claims that 'there is a broad consensus among researchers and education/training practitioners in Britain that the most powerful disincentive to train is the potential risk of benefit entitlement and a precarious financial stability' McGivney (1992, p8).

McGivney and others have shown that claimants were reluctant to change their benefit status due to the bureaucratic difficulties which may arise and the possible loss of benefit. As a tutor on a course for the unemployed said: 'The view is, once you've got benefit sorted out, don't touch it, especially if the course is only for a few weeks' (quoted in McGivney, 1992). In addition, as a report by the People and Work Unit (1990) indicated, 'any potential changes constitute a threat to adapted regimes, renegotiated family roles, and to security of income and benefits, however, low' (People and Work Unit, 1990).

In other words, although claimants can mix benefits and work or benefits and trainee allowances, the perceived risks are often too great, and short-run imperatives take precedence. In the case of training, there is also the added uncertainty of whether or not it would lead to a better job or increase employability. The fears of putting a stable benefit position at risk and the increasing difficulty of finding a job, many of which are insecure, combine to 'immobilise' unemployed people. Superimposed upon this are issues related to lack of confidence resulting from the experience of being unemployed.

As we have seen, the training allowances on government training programmes have not kept pace with inflation. Their low level may well act as a disincentive. For those on Employment Training, the additional £10 on top of benefit may not be sufficient to act as a motivator (Lindley, 1991, in McGivney, 1992).

Recent research had also shown how the '16 hour rule' adds to the financially precarious position of the unemployed. Garner and Imeson (1996), in their survey of 58 Access tutors working in Greater London and the South East, found that over 70 per cent of them felt that the introduction of the '16 hour rule' would result in more students having to make a choice between benefit and study and that it would severely affect recruitment. It was believed that the new rule would change the class balance of successful entrants. Only those who could afford to study would be able to participate. In addition, many non-traditional students often need additional support on literacy and numeracy and this may be unlikely within the reduced hours.

What is the impact on employed people?

But even employed people may be deterred from participating in further education and training due to financial reasons. In those instances where the employer is unwilling or unable to provide financial support, employees are at a disadvantage. This is particularly the case for part-time workers. In part, their lack of access arises from their position in the occupational hierarchy and whether or not they already possess educational qualifications. As already suggested, those workers most likely to receive such employer sponsored education and training are in higher level, skilled, well-paid, and stable jobs. As Gallie and White (1993, p30) observed from their survey of 3,855 people in work: 'People without educational qualifications had training less than half as frequently as those with qualifications.' Part-time jobs tend to be low-paid and unskilled. Employers tend to be unwilling to invest in such jobs and to incur both the direct and indirect costs of training.[21] Indeed, research (Callender and Metcalf, 1997) clearly shows that the key factors which reduce women's[22] chances of training are:

- being employed part-time
- being married or cohabiting
- having children under 5 years old.

Similarly, some employers are unwilling to invest in older workers and those on short-term contracts as they do not believe they will get a return on their investment.

---

21 The time part-timers spend away from work on off-the-job training is 'non-productive' and forms a greater proportion of their working time compared to full-time workers.

22 According to the Labour Force Survey, nearly 90 per cent of all part-time workers are women.

Approximately 15 per cent of the economically active fund their own training and the majority of these are in full-time jobs (Tremlett et al, 1995). Research suggests that the most significant factor affecting the likelihood that people will fund their own training is the age they completed their full-time education. Self-funders were more likely to have finished their education aged 17 or over than were other learners (Tremlett et al, 1995). Indeed, Gallie and White (1993) estimated that 'those with educational qualifications entered self-financed training three times as frequently as those without qualifications.' In other words, self-funding appears not to be a key option for widening participation in terms of encouraging individuals who have never been involved in further education participate.

According to De Bell and Davies (1991) individuals' reluctance to be self-funding is associated with the costs. They suggest that release from work may become a problem, especially as the training programmes tend to be designed to fit conventional weekday schedules. Indeed, recent research on part-time students in higher education clearly shows that students who were undertaking a qualification because it was a job requirement, were much more likely than others to have supportive employers who paid their fees and helped with the costs of their books, materials, and travel (Callender, 1997a).

4.7 SUMMARY

Financial support or the lack of it, are important determinants of access to further education and training, but they are one of several determinants. The limited research in Britain shows that financial support such as training allowances and fee remission policies are incentives to initial access. Conversely, the lack of such financial support is often cited as a disincentive especially for adults, unemployed people, and women. Barriers to participation include, tuition fees, the add-on costs of training and other indirect costs such as childcare.

Various national studies conducted in the United States have examined the enrolment behaviour of school leavers. These studies are primarily concerned with access to higher education which includes community colleges. The studies show unequivocally that financial aid has a positive impact on student enrolment, especially among students from low-income families.

There is a broad consensus in the American research that increases in tuition costs depress enrolment levels among students from low income groups but not those from high income groups. Similarly, research shows that financial aid packages which include monies for maintenance also have a positive impact on enrolment, as do their value. Grants have been found to be a more effective recruitment tool than loans, especially for the lowest income groups.

There are multiple reasons why certain sections of society do not seek out or take up education and training. It is difficult to isolate any one factor, including financial support. The evidence from Britain seems to suggest that where structural, institutional and dispositional factors interact with practical concerns such as financial support, individuals are deterred from participation. However, evidence from the United States suggests that after social class and parental education, economic issues are a major determinant of participation.

Chapter 5

Financial support, retention and achievement

5.1 INTRODUCTION

The purpose of this chapter is to assess the role of financial support in students' retention and achievement in further education and training. It begins with a brief discussion of current retention and achievement levels in the sector and how these vary. It then considers the non-financial factors affecting completion and drop-out. Finally, it explores the extent to which financial support acts as an incentive to stay on and complete and, conversely, how the lack of such support and financial hardship works as a disincentive. It is within this context that the limitations of current research on retention, discussed in Chapter 3, are particularly pronounced.

5.2 WHAT ARE THE NON-COMPLETION LEVELS?

5.2.1 Why is non-completion a growing concern?

According to Martinez (1995a), it is only within the last five years that we have seen 'something of a revolution' in perspectives on retention. From a position of relative unimportance, issues around student retention now attract national prominence. This growing concern has been associated with several interrelated factors.

- Official concerns with the quality, effectiveness, and accountability of the further education sector, especially since incorporation, have led to greater monitoring of student progress. Indeed, of the six performance indicators applied to colleges in 1994/95, three specifically related to student numbers, retention, and outcomes.
- There are considerable financial costs associated with non-completion. The failure of an individual to achieve or complete means non-payment for the college (McGivney, 1996). Thus the funding of further education colleges has become increasingly linked to evidence of student attendance, completions and 'successful' outcomes. Indeed, it has been estimated that as much as £500 million in public funds are consumed in students who withdraw annually (Page, 1996).
- Students who do not complete their course can also incur considerable financial, social and personal costs.

However, some commentators (for example, McGivney, 1996) have suggested that it is the external pressures, rather than a consideration of the personal consequences of non-completion for students, that are forcing institutions to confront this issue.

5.2.2 What are the retention rates and how do they vary?

The latest available figures, based on individualised student records which are compiled by providers and collated by the FEFC, indicate that the overall level of retention is high in the sector for those enrolled on a full-year programme. In 1994/95, it stood at over 85 per cent in England. However, these rates vary slightly (Table 5.1) depending on a variety of factors.[23]

Table 5.1   Retention rates by whether students full or part-time and type of college

percentages

Type of college	Full-time students	Part-time students	All students
General	82	87	85
Tertiary	85	87	86
Sixth form	87	72	85
Other	86	85	86
Total	**84**	**86**	**85**

Source: derived from FEFC press release, September 1996

Retention rates vary by:

- *Students' age:* they are slightly higher for full time students under 19 (85 per cent) compared with those aged 19–59 (81 per cent) but the opposite is true for part-time students (84 per cent compared to 86 per cent).
- *Type of course:* overall, part-time students were very slightly more likely to complete than full-time students (Table 5.1).
- *Type of institution:* tertiary and other types of colleges had slightly higher rates than sixth form colleges or general colleges (Table 5.1). A recent FEFC report on A level and AS courses, based on inspection visits to 100 further education colleges in England, showed that there were differences in withdrawal rates among institutions. While some institutions, particularly sixth form colleges, had less than 10 per cent drop-out, others were experiencing drop-out of 15 per cent or more (FEFC, 1994).
- *Level of qualification:* generally, the higher the qualification, the higher the retention rate, so retention levels stood at 83 per cent for level 1 but rose to 90 per cent for level 4 and above (derived from FEFC, 1996d).
- *Type of qualification:* retention rates for all students have tended to be higher for those taking GSCE's and GCE A/AS levels (82 and 86 per cent respectively) than for those pursuing GNVQs and NVQs (level 2 GNVQ 75 per cent and NVQ 81 per cent; level 3 GNVQ 80 per cent and NVQ 86 per cent).

Other research, for example Robinson's (1996) analysis of data from an Audit Commission/ OFSTED (1993) study, which was based on a sample of 1764 students who enrolled on two-year A level courses, 924 students who enrolled on BTEC National courses, and 598 students who enrolled on BTEC First courses in a number of educational institutions, has also shown

---

23 It is not possible to discuss how these completion rates have changed over time as comparable data are not readily available.

differences by type of qualification. Robinson compared this data with completion rates for GNVQs provided by the NCVQ. He showed that completion rates were significantly lower for Advanced GNVQs in comparison to BTEC Nationals and A levels which GNVQs are displacing.

Robinson's work can, however, be criticised for comparing awards data with registrations for the year of assumed commencement of the course. Registrations are an unreliable measure of the number of students on courses. Students may switch courses, leave early on or not take up places.

When examining particular qualifications, the relationship between the level of qualification and completion rates discussed above, does not necessarily hold. Various studies (FEU et al, 1994; BTEC, 1995), have estimated GNVQ non-completion rates of around 20 per cent for Intermediate level courses, but 40 per cent for Advanced level courses.

5.2.3   What are the achievement rates and how do they vary?

Achievement rates are considerably lower than retention rates. For example, in 1994/95, according to data from the FEFC, the overall estimated achievement rate[24] stood at 65 per cent in England.[25] It varied, too, by the following:

- *Students' age:* it was higher for students under 19 (69 per cent) than for adult students, age 19–59 (63 per cent).
- *Type of course:* data by whether the student was studying full or part-time are not readily available. However, given the concentration of adult students in part-time education and vice versa, it could be inferred that achievement rates among part-time students was likely to be lower than for full-time students.
- *Type of college:* sixth form colleges (81 per cent) had the highest rates while general colleges (64 per cent) had the lowest.
- *Level of qualification:* once again, the higher the qualification, the higher the achievement rate so achievement levels stood at 62 per cent for level 1 but rose to 69 per cent for level 4 and above.
- *Type of qualification:* achievement rates for all students tended to be considerably lower for those pursuing an NVQ compared with those taking an GNVQ or GSCE and GCE A/AS levels. At level 2 the NVQ achievement rate was 56 per cent compared to a rate of 66 per cent for both GCSEs and GNVQs. At level 3 the achievement rate for NVQs dropped to 52 per cent compared with 67 per cent for GCE A/AS levels and 70 per cent for GNVQs.

5.2.4   What are some of the problems with the British studies on non-completion?

Before reviewing the studies on the role of finance and drop-out, it is worth reiterating a few methodological issues raised in Chapter 3. They have to be kept in mind when interpreting the findings of the studies reported in the remainder of this chapter. Most of the studies which have been conducted about non-completion have not included a group of current students or completers. The conclusions of these studies are therefore limited because they are based solely on the views of non-completers. Even where both completers and non-completers are included in a study, the two groups may have been given different types of questionnaires

---

24   The achievement rate is calculated by comparing the number of students achieving a qualification with the total number completing courses intended to lead to one.

25   It is not possible to discuss how these achievements have changed over time as comparable data are not readily available.

(see, for example, CSET, 1994). We can infer, therefore, from the data that *within* the groups of withdrawn students, certain factors were perceived to be important and contributed or else prompted the decision to withdraw. But we cannot draw any conclusions about the typicality of the withdrawn student within the student population as a whole. Nor can we identify which of the multiple reasons (both non-financial and financial) for withdrawal seem to have had most effect.

5.3 WHAT NON-FINANCIAL FACTORS AFFECT COMPLETION AND ACHIEVEMENT?

There are a number of non-financial factors which influence whether a student will stay on or drop out of further education and training. Taken together, these factors predispose individuals to drop out and help explain why they drop out. They can be categorised as structural, institutional, dispositional and situational.

5.3.1 Which structural factors affect completion?

Academic ability and social class are factors which predispose individuals to drop out. For example, Payne et al (1996) in their analysis of the Youth Cohort Survey found that those young people with poor GCSE results were more likely to drop out than those with good results. In turn, as suggested in the previous chapter, they found that prior achievement was strongly associated with the parental occupation of students.

Research from the United States similarly shows that the pre-college family income of college students is strongly correlated with the eventual success of students in college (Mumper and Vander Ark, 1991). Students from low-income families are less likely to finish college, and those who finish, are less likely to do well. Analysis of longitudinal databases which track students over time, has shown that six years after graduating from high school, 80 per cent of students from high-income families, but only 40 per cent from low-income families, who started college, had finished (Caroll, 1989). However, once other factors are controlled for, the direct impact of income on the attainment of an undergraduate degree is less pronounced (Velez, 1985). Bean (1985) also demonstrates that high school grades are a strong predictor of college grades, which in turn predict retention. College grades are a much stronger predictor in the retention of first and second year undergraduates than those in their third year (and later).[26]

Academic ability can be a significant factor in explaining drop-out in terms of failure during the course. For instance, a recent study showed that 17 per cent of those taking a part-time course and 24 per cent taking a full-time course had withdrawn because they had failed assessments and found the course too hard. In this particular study it was the single most frequently mentioned reason for dropping out. In addition, a further 16 per cent of part-timers and 11 per cent of full-time students withdrew because they had obtained poor grades (BTEC, 1993). Bale's (1990) study similarly demonstrates that some 18 per cent of students had withdrawn because they failed their assessment, but it was only the fourth most frequently mentioned reason for non-completion.

In both these studies, however, it is difficult to ascertain what actually caused the failure and poor grades. Failure can be associated with the student's academic ability. It can be traced back to poor performance in school and low academic ability. But, as is well established, failure can be related to a range of other factors, especially institutional and dispositional factors – discussed below. In addition, as Martinez (1995b) has observed in his review of several major studies on drop-out, some of the key studies (for example,

---

26 In the United States most undergraduate degrees are four-year courses.

HMI/DES, 1991; FEU, 1994a) did not ask students about failed assessments. Nor did they have comparative groups who were asked similar questions.

Employment status and the state of the labour market have also been found to be very important explanations for non-completion. In Sharp's (1996) review of a range of studies on non-completion, she concluded that employment related factors accounted for between a third and a half of all withdrawals.

As discussed in Chapter 4, there is evidence to suggest that when the labour market is tight, young people will stay on in post-compulsory education. However, some of these students may not be fully committed, and so when employment opportunities arise, they leave to take them up. Unwin (1995) refers to this as the 'labour market pull'.

The labour market pull is particularly strong for full-time students. Analyses of the Youth Cohort Study (Payne, 1995) show that of students who dropped out of A level and AS level courses within the first year and left full-time education, about half went into full-time jobs in 1990. However, this proportion fell to less than a third in 1993.

Getting a full-time job was the most frequently mentioned reason for non-completion in a recent FEU (1994a) study of full-time further education college students (27 per cent gave this reason). It was the second most frequently mentioned reason given by students in Smith and Bailey's (1993) study of BTEC students (18 per cent gave this reason).

Both HMI (1991) and Smith and Bailey (1993) point out that part-time students are particularly affected by changes to their employment circumstances, which may cause them to leave their course before completion. The HMI (1991) study, based on the completion rates of 12 further education colleges in different parts of England, showed that 15 per cent of students withdrew due to 'changes relating to employment', such as redundancy, changes of duties, shift work, or change of location. The demands of employment also had a considerable impact on many of the part-time students' ability to complete a course requiring regular attendance over one or two years. Similarly, Smith and Bailey (1993) reported that changes in employment and other work-related pressures were among the main reasons for part-time BTEC students to leave early, with 19 per cent citing these reasons. Medway and Penney (1994) also found that the pressure of work led to withdrawal. Those students who were working very long hours found it difficult to sustain their studies due to the competition for time from part-time work.

5.3.2 Which institutional factors affect completion?

As indicated in Table 5.1 the level of retention varies with the type of institution which in turn suggests that what happens in colleges, especially organisational and course-related factors, can affect non-completion.

Organisational factors influence completion/non-completion. These include issues such as:

- the appropriateness of the match between student and course;
- the quality of induction;
- the student's experiences of teaching and learning;
- tutorial support and timetabling.

The appropriateness of the match between the student and their course has, in turn, been associated with several factors (Sharp, 1996). The importance of these issues is that together they may well contribute to students failing their course and thus becoming disenchanted and demotivated, and so influence their decision to withdraw.

- Inappropriate course placement: Medway and Penney (1994) in their study of 498 students at the Isle of Wight College, found that a third of students who had withdrawn from vocational courses felt that they had enrolled on the wrong level programme.

- Subject choice: a recent FEFC study (FEFC, 1994) showed that in one of the colleges studied, 40 per cent of the students who were well advanced in their A level courses would with hindsight have chosen different subjects.

- The absence of specific entry criteria: another FEFC report on GNVQs, based on inspection visits to 114 further education colleges showed that as a result of this, some students had been inappropriately placed on intermediate programmes. Consequently they left early and failed to achieve the qualification.

- Poor quality advice coming from inappropriate sources: Medway and Penney (1994) found that 65 per cent of non-completers had received their initial information from sources other than the college. The quality of guidance and information before coming to college was a source of dissatisfaction for both completers and non-completers.

  However, students sometimes reject good quality guidance from tutors about the choice of an appropriate course. Green and Ainley (1995) in their research on post-16 education and training, based on interviews with senor managers in 10 institutions (including seven further education institutions and three schools), found this to be the case. A major concern for staff was that some students, with little chance of success, were insistent on enroling for A level courses, because of the perceived 'currency' of this qualification.

The quality of induction can affect completion. Particularly significant is the role of induction in integrating new students into the institution. Unwin's (1995) study, which involved interviews with 120 full-time students in South and East Cheshire, showed that some students found it difficult to establish a sense of belonging and had problems relating to other students. This contributed to their decision to leave. Similarly, Medway and Penney's (1994) study 'strongly suggested that 'something' in the introductory and induction phases worked less well for non-completing students'(Martinez, 1995a, p10). Ninety-two per cent of those completing the course felt welcome when they first came to their college compared to 67 per cent of non-completers. Indeed, non-completion was correlated with a number of factors associated with induction and integration into programmes and into the college generally.

The experiences of teaching and learning have been shown to affect completion. Research on the differences between completers and non-completers demonstrates that they have significantly different experiences of teaching and learning. In Medway and Penney's (1994) study, for example, withdrawn students were more likely than those who completed their course to be dissatisfied with the amount of tutorial time they had received (66 per cent compared to 27 per cent). In addition, non-completers were less likely to be satisfied with the level at which the course was pitched; with the speed and pace of teaching; and with the level of interest sustained by the course.

Timetabling and student support have also been identified as contributing to non-completion. The results of Medway and Penney's (1994) study showed that long days and long gaps between classes made it difficult for students to meet paid work and college commitments, as well as family responsibilities. This situation was exacerbated by the travel problems experienced by some non-completers. In addition, as Page (1996, p15) pointed out in her recent study of student support services, 'all the providers of student services were convinced that good welfare provision improved retention and that was ultimately its raison d'être'. However, it is sometimes the case that members of staff are unable, due to time constraints, or ill equipped, due to their lack of the necessary expertise, to provide adequate support.

Course-related factors also contribute to non-completion (Medway and Penney, 1994; Green and Ainley, 1995; Unwin, 1995), but Sharp (1996) in her review of the literature suggests that the importance ascribed to them varies. For example, the HMI (1991) study, which reported on a range of reasons for non-completion in a variety of further education courses, found that only 10 per cent of withdrawals were due to dissatisfaction with the course or to poor progress. In contrast, FEU (1994a) research on full-time courses carried out in West Suffolk estimated that about a third of withdrawals occurred for this reason. And Smith and Bailey (1993) showed that 44 per cent of withdrawals from BTEC courses took place for course-related reasons.

Some of the course-related factors include:

- The lack of basic skills: Green and Ainley (1995), for example, found that some students lacked the necessary skills in Mathematics, English and independent study which contributed to their lack of progress and ultimately, to drop-out. Unwin (1995) also found that a lack of independent skills contributed to the decision by students to withdraw while the FEFC (1994) referred to student problems with mathematics as a reason for non-completion.
- The course content: Unwin (1995) reported that some students withdrew because they found the content of the course was not what they had expected or because it did not match with their previous experience.
- Students' difficulty in adapting to teaching styles in further education compared to the more didactic styles they had experienced at school.
- Problems with assessment (FEFC, 1994) and concerns about the emphasis on terminal written examinations in A level courses (Green and Ainley, 1995).

What these organisational and course-related factors highlight is that colleges have considerable scope for influencing the extent of withdrawal among their students.

5.3.3 Which dispositional factors affect completion?

Like access to further education and training, the students' attitudes, level of motivation and confidence can influence whether or not they stay on. Green and Ainley (1995) found that some of the students who had withdrawn from A level courses had lost their motivation and interest. And as we will see, these issues have been found to be of particular importance in the studies on persistence in the United States. However, British research suggests that other factors such as lack of finance, are usually cited to mask students' negative attitudes, lack of motivation and confidence.

5.3.4 Which situational factors affect completion?

As Sharp (1996) pointed out, estimates of the extent to which personal difficulties such as family demands, health, and accommodation influence non-completion vary considerably. For example, the HMI (1991) study showed that about 40 per cent of withdrawals were due to personal reasons, while FEU (1994a), based on information from the study in West Suffolk, found that 30 per cent of early leavers dropped out because of personal reasons. These studies, by highlighting these types of issues, place the onus of responsibility for withdrawal on the individual.

Problems with accommodation were raised by non-completing students interviewed by Unwin (1995) and Medway and Penney (1994). There was a link between the lack of money and the ability to afford suitable accommodation. In addition, some students who wanted to leave their family homes, could not do so, due to the lack of money. This sometimes led to conflicts with parents and siblings.

Family problems suffered by early leavers include family breakdown, bereavement, and needing to care for a family member. Students also had family commitments and responsibilities which led to absenteeism, so they fell behind with their work, and this too contributed to withdrawal. Physical and mental health problems, as well as pregnancy, have also been documented as reasons for withdrawal (Medway and Penney, 1994). The Isle of Wight study also pointed out that while a higher proportion of completers than non-completers said that they had personal and health problems while at College, whether or not the students withdrew depended on the extent and nature of the difficulties; the help they received; and the effect on their college work (Medway and Penney, 1994).

Lack of time arising out of domestic responsibilities and work schedules can also affect retention particularly for women, given that they tend to have prime responsibility for domestic duties and a disproportionate number of them work part-time. Further, inadequate transport and lack of childcare provision may also feed into the decision to withdraw, particularly among women.

Finally, financial support or the lack of it can influence completion/non-completion – the following sections look at this in more detail.

5.4   DOES FINANCIAL SUPPORT ACT AS AN INCENTIVE?

5.4.1   What is the evidence from British studies?

There is limited evidence available in Britain to suggest that financial support can have a positive impact on retention and completion. A recent evaluation of Career Development Loans found that as many as 80 per cent of trainees completed their courses (IFF, 1994). However, from the data available, it is not possible to confirm whether the loans acted as a positive incentive to complete and if so, how. Individuals who take out these loans undertake a variety of different qualifications, and as we have seen, completion rates vary considerably by the type of qualification. So in order to see if CDLs acted as a positive incentive to complete, we would need to compare the completion rates of individuals taking a particular qualification with those not in receipt of a CDL, but pursuing a similar qualification.

The HMI's (1993) study of adults in further education during the academic year 1991/92 showed that where courses were sponsored, for example by TECs, completion rates were relatively high. It is also suggested (for example, De Bell, 1993) that students sponsored by their employers tend to have higher completion rates than those who are not. However, it may not be the sponsorship per se which leads to higher completion rates. As research on part-time students in higher education shows (Callender, 1997a), employers who sponsor their employees are more encouraging and supportive than employers who do not offer such help.

5.4.2   What is the evidence from American studies?

As we have seen, non-completion tends to be higher among students from low-income families. Studies conducted in the United States reveal that financial aid can have a positive impact on 'persistence' in terms of countering the impact of disadvantage associated with low income. For instance, it has shown how students who receive means-tested student aid are as likely to persist as more affluent students (Stampen and Cabrera, 1986; 1988).

Those studies in the United States which are based on econometric analyses of large datasets and model the effects of receiving aid on persistence for different types of students, also show that financial aid positively affects retention. These econometric studies clearly demonstrate that the costs associated with pursuing a college education influence individuals' 'persistence decisions'.

The studies use persistence models which usually examine the relationships between background, achievement, college experiences, student financial aid and whether students persist from one semester to another, or complete their first year. And just as recent American studies on enrolment have adopted a differentiated-price approach, by attempting to disentangle the impact of tuition fees, maintenance grants, and loans, so too have studies on drop-out.

For instance, Astin (1975, 1982) concluded that grants and work-study programmes were beneficial for persistence, but loans were not. Somers (1995) traced the progress of first-year students who had enrolled in 1989 at an urban institution that offered scholarships to a small number of applicants. She found that there were significant associations between students completing their first year of academic study and their receipt of student financial aid. She concluded that the total amount of aid offered was significant in promoting persistence among all students. In addition, the amount of both grants and loans affected persistence among low-income students. However, where a grant and loan were differentiated by the same amount ($1,000), grants increased the probability of completion more than loans. In other words, grants were a more effective retention tool than loans.

Somers (1995) also observed that longer-term persistence, namely year-to-year persistence, was affected by other factors apart from student aid. Thus money may not be as important as the 'fit' between the student and their institution in understanding why students do not re-enrol after completing their first year of study. However, St John (1990) in an earlier study, which examined the year-to-year persistence decisions by college students from the high-school class of 1980, came to somewhat different conclusions to Somers. This may be because his work was based on a nationally representative group of students while Somers relied on students from just one educational institution. St John found that students were influenced by tuition charges, and student aid award amounts, in their persistence decisions. His analysis showed that students' decisions were affected by the amount of all types of student aid awarded, and that awards had a larger influence than tuition charges on their decisions.

An important feature of more recent research (St John and Starkey, 1995) in the United States has been to highlight how students view prices differently when making decisions to enter higher education and when deciding to withdraw. Moreover, it is the combination of prices they face which impact on their decisions. The significance of this distinction emerges in the St John and Starkey (1995) analysis of the National Post-secondary Education Student Aid Survey of 1986–87 which includes a national sample of all undergraduate students. While the amount of grant awarded to low-income students had a positive impact on their *enrolment* decision, it had a negative impact on their *persistence.* In other words, the larger their grant the greater the likelihood that individuals would enter higher education. However, once an individual had enrolled as a student, they found that they had insufficient resources to persist. So although the grants encouraged initial participation among low-income students, where they were too low, they contributed to student drop-out.

Furthermore, St John and Starkey (1995) suggest that the relative importance of various types of prices and subsidies is also determined by the choices students make and other factors, such as the reasons they choose to attend a college. In other words, how students respond to tuition fees or student aid in their persistence decision, is probably affected by, and interacts with, issues like their preferences.[27]

5.5   DOES THE LACK OF FINANCIAL SUPPORT ACT AS A DISINCENTIVE?

5.5.1   What is the evidence from British studies?

How important is financial support?

The importance attributed to the lack of financial support and financial hardship in non-completion varies. Thus, Sharp's (1996) literature review of completion rates of A level and GNVQ courses devotes little discussion to this issue. Turning to actual empirical studies on

---

27 These types of contributory factors to drop-out have been explored in much more depth by the sociological literature in the United States. The findings of these students will be discussed in the next section.

non-completion, at one end of the spectrum there are studies which ignore the issue completely. For instance, Bale (1990) did not give the people she surveyed the opportunity to identify finance as a reason for withdrawal.[28] Other studies ascribe very little significance, if any, to financial reasons relative to other factors. For example, in Cass's study (1994) of 50 sixth form college students, none of the students cited financial reasons as a basis for non-completion. This may be because of the type of students and the type of institution they attended. In the Youth Cohort Survey a special additional survey conducted in 1994/95 asked full-time students why they failed to complete their course. Analysis of their responses revealed seven categories of reasons, but finance was not one of them.

Smith and Bailey's (1993) study of over 2,000 BTEC students on full-time and part-time programmes also showed that financial reasons, unlike other factors, were not highly significant for the majority of students examined. It indicated that only 3 per cent of part-time students and 5 per cent of full-time students cited financial reasons as the cause of non-completion. By contrast, 31 per cent of part-timers and 19 per cent of full-time students had not completed their programmes for employment-related reasons. The HMI (1991) study, based on the college records of 260 full-time and part-time students, identified only two per cent of students who had referred to financial reasons. Again, this reason was the least likely of all reasons to have been identified as causing drop-out. In contrast, those related to employment, family/health and other reasons accounted for nearly two out of five reasons identified. It is important to note, however, that this particular study is based on college records which were completed by staff rather than by the students themselves (see Chapter 3).

In the Isle of Wight study of just over a hundred college students, the main reasons why students decided to leave related to organisational and course-related factors such as inadequacies in pre-course contact, induction, classroom experience and the college environment. Financial reasons ranked the second most important reasons. However, three and half times as many students mentioned organisational and course related reasons as mentioned financial reasons (Medway and Penney, 1994).

By contrast, at the other end of the spectrum, other studies stress the importance of financial hardship as a major cause of withdrawal. The Staff College research of 85 full-time college students, for example, showed that as many as 22 per cent of them cited financial reasons as the cause of withdrawal (CSET, 1994). It was the joint second most frequently mentioned reason after family and health reasons.

Only the last two of the studies reported above included both current students and those who had withdrawn. Thus it is only from these studies that we can really assess the importance of financial issues relative to other factors leading to withdrawal. They indicate that finance related issues do not help particularly to distinguish withdrawn from current students. For example, in Medway and Penney's (1994) study of the Isle of Wight College, the percentage of students who said that they had difficulty paying for a bus pass was virtually the same in both groups. The proportion of completing students who indicated that they were receiving assistance from the benefit system was rather more than twice the proportion of withdrawn students.

The Staff College Research (1994) also showed similar results. Financial hardship and the lack of financial assistance received the highest ratings from the whole group of respondents as reasons for withdrawal. Current students, however, felt that these factors applied to them at least as much as to withdrawn students. The only statistically significant reason which applied more to withdrawn students was that the 'college did not care'. The withdrawn students had a significantly lower opinion of the college than current students in terms of how they rated the quality of the staff and the help they received (Martinez, 1995a, p13).

---

28 Bale did, however, have an 'other reasons' category which included, among others, financial reasons.

This research has reinforced the conviction that curbing student drop-out needs a college-wide approach to tackling the issue (Spours, 1997, p62). It also suggests that financial issues alone, are unlikely to lead to drop-out. However when financial hardship or a lack of financial support are combined with other factors, then drop-out may well occur.

What type of financial hardship do individuals experience?

Although many studies have examined whether financial hardship is a contributory factor in the decision to withdraw, very few have explored the nature of the financial hardship experienced; what exactly caused the hardship; how students coped with hardship; and the implications of hardship for their educational experience.

Bryant and Noble (1989), however, in their study of students on a particular course at Ruskin College between 1981 and 1986, showed that at the personal level, financial hardship led to 20 per cent of students cutting back on the purchase of food and making economies in social and leisure activities. The authors also found 'clear evidence that the incidence and scale of debt has increased over the years' (Bryant and Noble, 1989, p339). For many, financial difficulties affected the quality of their educational experience: books and other materials could not be purchased; the choice of placements was limited by financial considerations; having to work during term-time interfered with studies; and anxieties about debt undermined morale.

The FEU's (1993) small-scale qualitative study of 57 self-funded learners from ten colleges which tracked their progress over a year, highlighted some of the serious financial issues these students faced. These students relied on a variety of sources of income. Some 20 per cent had received a grant of some kind and over a half had had to pay fees. Many of the students complained of the shortage of money and the loss of social life, in particular. Others were unhappy about the incompatibility of benefit entitlement and local authority grants, while others faced severe hardship especially in the summer break of a two-year course.

The Wirral Metropolitan College (1993) study revealed that many students who were supported by discretionary grants, experienced financial difficulties because they were not used to budgeting with three lump sums per year. In the past, they had tended to budget weekly or monthly. Those who were in receipt of social security benefit also did not realise that they would lose their passport benefits, like free school meals for their children, after receiving the grant.

5.5.2 What is the evidence from American studies?

Sociological studies conducted in the United States look more broadly at why students leave higher education and they locate the influence of financial aid within this broader decision-making context. In other words, they tend to give deeper insights into how financial and non-financial factors interact to cause drop-out.

Some of the most seminal work in the United States on student drop-out has been conducted by Tinto (1975; 1982; 1987). Building on Spady's (1970; 1971) work, Tinto developed a model for explaining the process that motivates individuals to leave higher education before graduating. He suggested that students drop out when there is a 'lack of congruence or mismatch between the individual and the institution' (Tinto, 1993, p51). He suggests that persistence is a function of the match between a student's motivation and academic ability and the institution's academic and social characteristics. This interaction in turn, impacts on and shapes two underlying individual commitments: to completing college (the goal commitment) and to a student's particular college (institutional commitment). Thus retention and drop-out result from the interactions between students and colleges. Students who persist are said to 'fit' while those who leave exhibit 'a lack of fit'.

A key drawback with Tinto's original model is that it did not consider the importance of external factors on persistence, including the role of student finance. His more recent analyses have considered this. He concluded (Tinto, 1993) that the main effects of student aid occurred when individuals were deciding whether to attend college and where to enrol. For most students, financial aid had a marginal effect on the decision to leave college.

More recent studies suggest that financial aid has a significant total effect on persistence, but only indirectly (Cabrera el al, 1992; 1993). Cabrera el al (1993) show that the strongest factor directly impacting on persistence was the students' intention to continue studying, followed by their academic scores over the year. In turn, students' intentions to continue studying in the next academic year were most heavily influenced by their commitment to their institution and the encouragement they received from family and friends to continu attending. In explaining the indirect role of financial aid they suggest: 'The results specifically underline the indirect nature of finances in the persistence process in that it affects the student's academic integration, socialisation processes, as well as his or her resolve to persist in college' (Cabrera el al, 1992, p589).

5.6 HOW DOES THE LACK OF FINANCIAL SUPPORT AFFECT PARTICULAR GROUPS OF STUDENTS?

5.6.1 How does the lack of financial support affect mature and younger students?

Mature students are more likely than younger ones to leave courses for reasons that are external to the course or institution, including financial hardship. The Wirral Metropolitan College (1993) study, for example, showed that personal and other reasons for leaving were more likely to be given by older students, while younger students were more likely to leave for job-related reasons.

In addition, several studies have found that financial difficulties tend to be more acute among mature students. For example, Cullen's (1994) study of access students revealed 'how hard it is to be a mature student with no financial backing in the form of a grant and no childcare provision or allowance'. It is not surprising, therefore, that these older students linked their withdrawal to financial issues.

Reports provided by several Access Validating Agencies for McGivney's (1996) research into retention stressed the role of 'problems with finance' in decisions to withdraw by mature Access students. The HMI (1993) study of adults in further education similarly showed that financial hardship was often the cause of students not completing their course, particularly on part-time Access courses.

A number of in-house college studies of adult students also emphasise financial reasons (Wirral Metropolitan College, 1993). The small-scale survey conducted at Kensington and Chelsea College (1995) among full-time students, the majority of whom were over 21, showed that 60 per cent of those leaving the course said that they made this decision because of financial reasons. A survey at the same college among 100 part-time students, most of whom were over 25, showed that one third of them found finance a problem. A student counsellor involved in McGivney's (1996) project on retention claimed that as many as 90 per cent of the people he sees, and who subsequently leave their course of study, have financial problems.

There is much less hard evidence that younger students experience such problems but their potential financial hardship should not be discounted. It is likely that their problems will be hidden as the financial hardship is born by their nuclear family. The landmark study of student retention and non-completion by the Audit Commission/OFSTED (1993) indicated that financial hardship was one of the factors which contributed significantly to drop-out among 16–18 year olds on full-time courses.

5.6.1 How does the lack of financial support affect unemployed and employed students?

Unemployed students are also more likely than their employed counterparts to be adversely affected by a lack of financial support. A study of unemployed adults who had withdrawn from a further education college in Gloucestershire showed that the problems experienced by these students while studying were predominantly financial (69 per cent), with the costs of examination fees, books and childcare also being mentioned (Dekker and Whitfield, 1989).

It is believed that the new 16 hour rule will have a negative effect on drop-out, although no formal evaluation of its impact has been conducted. Certainly research has shown that the precursor to this, the 21 hour rule, has negatively affected drop-out (Finn, 1995; Garner and Imeson, 1996). The findings of these studies have been reported in Chapter 2 and will not be repeated here. One respondent remarked in anticipation of the new 16 hour rule that 'part-time students on fewer hours will have less commitment to the course and college, they will be less likely to identify with a group and so more likely to drop out' (Donnelly, 1997, p16).

There are few studies which specifically discuss the interplay between financial support and those in employment.

5.7 CONCLUSION

Research on the inter-relationship between drop-out and financial support has been conducted in Britain and the issue has become increasingly important with changes in the funding and inspection frameworks of colleges. There are, however, severe limitations to these studies. In particular, explanations for drop-out are often not based on students' own assessments and the circumstances of students dropping-out are not compared with those who do not.

The conclusion of these studies is that there is no single cause of drop-out. Diverse factors affect various groups of students differently, in disparate organisational contexts. More significant, financial hardship is just one of many complex factors contributing to drop-out. When experienced in conjunction with course-related factors such as dissatisfaction with the quality of teaching and learning support, drop-out is more likely to occur. This is reassuring in the sense that colleges and educational institutions can make a substantial difference to student outcomes by focusing on the quality of teacher-student interactions (Martinez, 1995b). However, McGivney (1996) warns of the dangers of separating these extrinsic and intrinsic factors.

Sociological studies in the United States have reached fairly similar, but more robust, conclusions. Most see attrition as attributed to a lack of congruency between students and their institutions. Financial aid has a significant total effect on persistence but only indirectly, by facilitating the 'fit' between students and their institutions. Such studies have also very importantly shown that financial aid can counter the impact of disadvantage associated with low income. Hence, students who receive means-tested student aid are as likely to persist as more affluent students.

Other types of research in the United States have modelled the interplay between persistence and financial support and show a positive association between financial assistance and retention rates, especially when models separate out the effects of tuition costs and various forms of financial aid. However, students respond differently to cost issues when considering their initial enrolment and when making decisions about dropping out. Insufficient funds do lead to non-completion or to breaks in study especially when tuition fees are high. One of the unintended consequences of this is to increase the time it takes for students to obtain their qualification.

Chapter 6

Learning accounts

6.1 INTRODUCTION

This chapter explores the current models for learning accounts which have been proposed by various organisations and individuals aimed at promoting 'lifelong learning'. The different models are described and their limitations highlighted.

6.2 WHAT ARE THE ORIGINS OF THE LEARNING ACCOUNTS?

The role of education and training in helping to promote national competitiveness and a flexible labour force has long been on the economic, social and political agenda. In recent years there have been numerous government initiatives aimed at placing this higher up those agendas.[29] Policy makers and others have sought to establish a society based on 'lifelong learning' – a Learning Society. In particular, they have attempted to place education higher up individuals' personal agenda, while at the same time shifting the burden of financial responsibility for education and training on to individuals. And in some ways they have succeeded – participation rates in post-compulsory education have never been higher. How can participation and provision be further expanded to the extent advocated by some commentators?

This report has clearly shown that the ability of individuals to participate in education and training is affected by their access to resources and by the prospects of indebtedness. Research shows, however, the unwillingness of some undergraduate students to take up student loans, especially women and Asians, because of the fear of debt and a dislike of borrowing (Payne and Callender, 1997; Callender and Kempson, 1996), while the American literature demonstrates that loans do not encourage enrolment especially when compared to grants (St John, 1993). This study has also shown how the current system of funding is unfair and fails to treat all types of learners equally. Full-time students in HE have access to a comprehensive range of financial support unlike part-time students in HE and all students in FE. The current provision favours young, full-time, academic learners while penalising adult, part-time and vocationally-focused learners.

---

29 Numerous initiatives could be cited, from the establishment of National Targets for Education and Training in 1991, to the reform of vocational qualifications with the introduction of National Vocational Qualifications and General National Vocational Qualifications.

These issues bring into question whether it is indeed possible to develop a 'Learning Society' and increase participation without a considerable increase in funding. In turn, this raises other questions. How should any expansion in supply be funded and who should pay? Should the State be the key purchaser of further education? And if they retain this role, is it possible for further education to expand to meet the increasing demand?

One potential solution is to build new 'learning investment coalitions' (Robertson, 1995). Such coalitions would bring together the state, employers and individuals to pay for individuals' education. And according to Robertson (1995) whose work has concentrated on higher education, this should be done through a balanced commitment which reflects the ratio of social to private rates of return to investment in post-compulsory and higher education. In other words, 'there should be a closer fit between private returns to higher education and the private costs; ipso facto for social returns and costs' (Robertson, 1995, p54). These ideas underpin the notion of learning accounts.

Learning accounts have gained support from a variety of sources such as the National Committee of Inquiry into Higher Education, chaired by Sir Ron Dearing, the FEFC's Widening Participation Committee chaired by Helena Kennedy and the Labour Party. It is likely, therefore, that they will attract considerable exposure and comment in the near future.

The principles informing learning accounts are sound and conceptually, they do have considerable potential. However, all the various interesting proposals as currently formulated have considerable drawbacks. Most of all, they are vague and poorly conceived.

6.3 WHAT ARE THE DIFFERENT MODELS OF LEARNING ACCOUNTS?

6.3.1 The Commission on Social Justice

The Commission on Social Justice (1994) outlined the idea of a Learning Bank as the framework for funding 'lifelong learning'. The strategy would be held together by a national qualification and credit framework. Its key features are as follows:

- Instead of the traditional emphasis on young academic students, the Learning Bank would be available throughout individuals' lives and allow them to learn when and how they like.
- The accumulation of credits by students through a modular system would drive the system. The credits would form the building blocks of lifetime learning and create a 'ladder of progression' through further education, higher education and vocational learning.
- Everyone would have an individual learning account at the Learning Bank to which government, individuals and employers could contribute while public money could lever private money into investing in learning.

Although the role of the Treasury is acknowledged, the nature of that role is not spelt out except that the Bank would exist independently of the Treasury. Nor are details about the scale or nature of employer and employee contributions outlined in detail. Indeed, the Report (1994, p414) admits: 'At the moment the learning Bank exists as a concept. Its organisation, and the details of its funding, structure and other matters, need to be developed more fully'.

Fairly similar, skeletal proposals have also been put forward by the National Commission on Education (1995).

6.3.2 The Labour Party

The Labour Party has subsequently developed the ideas put forward by the Commission on Social Justice. They included the idea of learning accounts in their 1997 election manifesto. They proposed the following (Full Employment, 1995).[30]

- Every employer would be required by law to contribute £2 a week into the learning account of all their employees who earn above the PAYE threshold.
- All employees above the PAYE threshold would have an account with the Learning Bank and would be required to contribute a minimum of £1 per week. Their contribution would be deducted at source by their employer.
- Employers and employees would jointly decide how the contributions were spent.

These proposals could generate a substantial investment in training among both employers and employees. There are, however, several drawbacks with these proposals as they stand at present:

- Certain groups of individuals will be excluded, that is those who do not contribute to PAYE, namely low-paid part-time workers many of whom are women, the self-employed, and the unemployed. All these groups need access to education and training.
- Each account will only be worth £156 per year. Consequently, the sort of education and training that could be purchased would be very limited. Indeed, given the level of contributions, these learning accounts alone would be insufficient to meet the costs of higher or further education. It is questionable how they will therefore achieve their aims of ensuring equitable access and funding to these forms of educational provision.
- They are likely to be very expensive and bureaucratic to administer and to have very high transitional costs. As Corney and Robinson (1995) have asked, how will the Learning Bank manage 21 million individual learning accounts and the 4.5 million job changes each year?[31]
- Employers will not necessarily be able to realise their investment in individuals, if the employee leaves. Therefore, companies with high turnover rates are particularly likely to be resistant to this proposal. Moreover, the increase in the wages bill resulting from the employers' contribution may well be passed on to employees as has happened with increases in National Insurance Contributions (Corney and Robinson, 1995).
- The employees' contributions are not income-related and the flat rate will act as a regressive tax with low-paid workers paying a higher proportion of their wage than higher paid workers.

6.3.3 The Liberal Democrats

The Liberal Democrats have made rather different proposals compared to the Labour Party. Implicit in their recommendations is a desire to deal with the inequitable funding between FE and HE and to tackle the flaws in the funding (Liberal Democrats, 1996).[32] They suggest that:

- Under their 'Learning Investment Partnerships' the government, employers and individual learners would contribute to the cost of education.
- Each person over 18 would be eligible to register at the Learning Bank by opening up an individual learning account. Students could debit their account to cover fees, living expenses, and course-related costs.

---

30 In the Labour Party manifesto the idea of learning accounts has been limited to up to level 3 only.

31 The costs of course would be less if the scheme is limited in the way proposed in the Labour Party manifesto.

32 The Liberal Democrat election manifesto flagged up somewhat less bold proposals.

- Government funding would be increased and some money allocated in the form of block grants as of present, while the remainder would be channelled through individual learning accounts.
- Employers' contributions would come from a 2 per cent remissible Education and Training Levy on company payrolls and provide the mechanism for employers to contribute to their employees' accounts.
- Individuals could build up and use their accounts whenever they wanted. If they borrowed more than the contribution made by the government, they would have to pay back the difference through the national insurance system once their earnings reached above a certain threshold.

The advantage of these proposals is that they attempt to integrate funding for further and higher education. However, the major drawbacks with these proposals are as follows:

- Training levies, in the past, have been particularly unpopular with employers and it is questionable whether these proposals are different enough to overcome the problems associated with them.
- As we have seen, some students are debt averse, they do not like to borrow, especially those from low-income families. They may, therefore, opt for the cheapest forms of education which may preclude certain types of further and higher education. Moreover, it is unclear whether the repayments on the loans from the Bank will be income contingent once individuals are earning above the threshold. Nor is it clear how long individuals will have to repay their loans.

6.3.4 Learning credits

Some of the ideas encapsulated in learning accounts are evident in the ideas underpinning learning credits or vouchers. These would provide young people with the means to purchase education and training, with public funds, directly from providers. Under the current proposals (Coopers and Lybrand, 1995), individuals would buy their education exclusively with public funds, young people would be the key beneficiaries, and the educational provision covered would be limited and exclude higher education, unlike some other models of learning accounts.

In their current form, learning credits are concerned primarily with empowering and motivating young people to participate in education, and increasing competition between providers. So their objective is to produce better, more cost-effective education and training. In other words, as conceived at the moment, they would not deal with the financial inequalities associated with access to different forms of educational provision. Moreover, they focus exclusively on the direct costs of provision rather than on costs associated with participation, including maintenance.

The current ideas do not, therefore, deal with key financial barriers to participation as highlighted in this report. However, given the importance attached to them by some commentators, it is worth briefly exploring some of the other drawbacks associated with them. More significant, some of their limitations are also applicable to learning accounts.

Various models of learning credits have been suggested (Coopers and Lybrand, 1995) including a cash-based credit system which would entitle young people to buy the learning provision of their choice, up to a maximum cash value specified on the credit. According to Cooper and Lybrand's report (1995), the main problem with this model is that:

- It would place considerable demands on young people, who would not only have to make judgements about the category and quality of their learning provision, but also value for money.

- This model, just like learning accounts, is predicated on a market-based approach yet currently there are considerable distortions and barriers to market operations.
- The cost of current provision varies enormously and so would its price. 'A simple flat rate cash could thus not support the current rate – unless it was set sufficiently high to cover the full range which would be extremely expensive in public expenditure terms' (Coopers and Lybrand, 1995, p5).

6.3.5   Other variations on a theme

Other commentators had proposed yet other models. For instance, Robertson (1996) has considered them in response to the funding crisis in higher education. He suggests that the idea of a Learning Bank 'which in partnership with the commercial banking sector, would be responsible for managing learning market transactions between individuals and institutional providers, based on a system of Individual Learning Accounts' (Robertson, 1996, p116). He estimates that it might cost £400 million to establish the Bank but it would generate £4 billion in new cash across the tertiary market over time.

Unlike other commentators, he envisages that the Bank could be constructed as a public authority but contracted out to the commercial banking sector. It would bear the risks of debt, or learning account overdrafts, in the absence of equivalent collateral. The government could establish fiscal initiatives like dedicated PEPs, TESSAs and bonds to encourage individual investment – another variation on the theme of Learning Bonds proposed by the AUT as a way of financing student loans (AUT, 1996).

The state, employers and individuals would contribute to the accounts, and in the spirit of perceiving education as a long-term investment, grandparents could also invest money in their grandchildren's accounts.

Robertson, has only partially addressed some of the practical issues by modelling different options (1996). For instance, in addressing the question of what machinery is needed so that individuals have access to and take responsibility for their learning account and its distribution, he proposes a quasi-market. However, many issues remained unresolved or unanswered. This is the major drawback with his proposals and other current proposals.

Many questions and issues remained unanswered and would need to be resolved. For example:

- How are employers to be persuaded to contribute voluntarily to learning accounts? Indeed what should be the balance between intervention and voluntarism for all contributors, not just employers?
- What incentives will individuals and others require to invest in these accounts? How are the contributions to be guaranteed, including the State's share?
- If employers are to invest more in education and training and be a key stakeholder, will they want to influence the nature of the education and training? Previous experience of such involvement, such as with the development of NVQs has proven to be highly problematic.
- How are the contributions to be collected and how is the system to be policed and defaulters dealt with?
- How is the Learning Bank to be managed? And what role, if any, will the Funding Councils, TECs, LEAs, Student Loan Company play?
- Would the learning accounts ultimately lead to the full privatisation of education and training?

A key challenge with learning accounts is that they are unknown territory. It is unknown what impact they would have on the supply of and demand for education; on standards; on the quality of education; and on whom the key beneficiaries would be in reality. These issues must be considered before the exciting concept is put into practice.

6.4   SUMMARY

Various interesting models of learning accounts or learning banks have been proposed by a range of organisations and individuals aimed at promoting 'lifelong learning'. Most suggest that the state, employers, and individuals should contribute to this account. It would be left to individuals to decide how to spend the monies in their account.

The precise focus, design, and operation of learning accounts is still to be defined. This makes it very difficult to assess their potential impact on increasing participation. However, any model which relies on contributions from employers or employees is likely to disadvantage the very groups most in need of further education and training – the unemployed, the self-employed and low-paid part-time workers.

The idea of learning accounts is an exciting one, and could potentially overcome many of the problems associated with the current financial support system. However, many questions are yet to be addressed especially the issue of, and concerns about, debt.

References

ACACE (1982) *Continuation Education: From Policies to Practice*, Leicester, ACACE

Adlington, E (1988) *Educational Vouchers for Unemployed Adults,* Leicester, NIACE/ REPLAN

ALFA (1987) *Annual Report 1986–87*, ALFA: Access to Learning for Adults, The North London Open College Network

Association of University Teachers (1996) *Funding: An approach to the National Committee of Inquiry into Higher Education,* London, AUT

Astin, A W (1975) *Preventing Students from Dropping Out*, San Francisco, Jossey-Bass

Astin, A W (1982) *Minorities in American Higher Education: Recent trends, current prospects and recommendations*, San Francisco, Jossey-Bass

Audit Commission/OFSTED (1993) *Unfinished Business: Full-time educational courses for 16-19 year olds*, London, HMSO

Baker, T and Velez, W (1996) Access to and opportunity in postsecondary education in the United States: A review, *Sociology of Education,* 82–101

Bale, E L (1990) *Student Drop-out from Part-time Course of Non-advanced Further Education,* Bedford CHE, M Phil thesis

Bean, J P (1985) Interaction effects based on class in an explanatory model of college student dropout syndrome, *American Educational Research Journal,* 22, 35–64

Boullen, K (1996) Individual learning accounts in practice, *Training Tomorrow,* 10 (5) 5–6

Bryant, R and Noble, M (1989) Grants, debts and second-chance students, *Adult Education* 61 (4) 336–341

BTEC (1993) *Staying the Course,* London, BTEC

BTEC (1995) *Shaping the Fut-ure: The BTEC Report 994,* London, BTEC

Cabrera, A F, Amaury, N and Castañeda, B (1992) The role of finances in the persistence process: A structural model, *Research into Higher Education*, 33, 571–93

Cabrera, A, Nora, A and Castañeda, B (1993) College persistence: structural equation modelling test of an integrated model of student retention, *Journal of Higher Education,* 64 (2) 123–139

Callender, C (1987) 'Women Seeking Work', in S Fineman et al (eds) *Unemployment. Personal and Social Consequences*, London and New York, Tavistock Publications

Callender, C (1997a) Full-time and part-time students in higher education: their experiences and expectations, *Higher Education in the Learning Society*, National Committee of Inquiry into Higher Education, Report 2, London, HMSO

Callender, C (1997b) *Individual Take-up of NVQs/SVQs: Stimuli and Obstacles*, Sheffield, Department for Education and Employment

Callender, C and Kempson, E (1996) *Student Finances: Income, Expenditure and Take-up of Student Loans*, London, Policy Studies Institute

Callender, C and Metcalf, H (1997) *Women and Training*, London, Policy Studies Institute

Cantor, L, Roberts, I and Pratley, B (1995) *A Guide to Further Education in England and Wales*, London, Cassell

Carroll, C D (1989) *College Persistence and Degree Attainment for 1980 High School Graduates: Hazards for Transfers, Stopouts and Part-timers,* Report No. Cs-89–302, Washington DC, National Centre for Education Statistics

Sir John Cass Foundation (1994) *Discretionary Award Provision in Inner London: Report of Main Findings and Conclusion*s, London, Sir John Cass Foundation

Charter, D (1995) Awards for Students Plummet, *The Times Higher Education Supplement,* 10 March, 5

Clotfelter, C (1993) 'Demand for Undergraduate Education', in C Clotfelter et al (eds) *Economic Challenges in Higher Education,* Chicago, University of Chicago

Coleman, J (1966) *Equality of Educational Opportunity*, Washington, US Office of Education

College Entrance Examination Board (1983) *Trends in Student Aid 1963–1983*, Washington DC

College Entrance Examination Board (1990) *Trends in Student Aid 1980–1990*, Washington DC

Commission on Social Justice (1994) *Social Justice: Strategies for National Renewal,* London, Vintage

Coopers & Lybrand (1995) *Learning Credits Consultancy Study*, London, Coopers & Lybrand

Corney, M and Robinson, P (1995) *Called to Account: Are compulsory individual learning accounts a wheeze or a nightmare?* London, Unemployment Unit

CSET Lancaster University (1994) *Quitting: A survey of early leaving carried out at Knowsley Community College,* unpublished

Cullen, M A (1994) *'Weighing it up': A case study of discontinuing access students*, University of Edinburgh, Centre for Continuing Education, Occasional Paper Series No 2

Daines, J, Elsey, B and Gibbs, M (1982) *Changes in Student Participation in Adult Education,* Nottingham, University of Nottingham

Darkenwald, G G (1988) *Comparison of Deterrents to Adult Education Participation in Britain and the United States*, SCUTREA

De Bell, D (1992) Paying for skills, *Adults Learning*, 4 (1) 7–9

De Bell, D (1993) Funding adult learning, *Training Officer,* 29 (3) 74–77

De Bell, D and Davies, B (1991) *Paying for Skills: Financial barriers to access to vocational training for adults*, Norwich, City College

Dekker, A and Whitfield, R (1989) *Completion Rates and Other Performance Indicators in Educational Opportunities for Unwaged Adults*, Leicester, NIACE REPLAN

Department for Education and Employment (1992) *Career Development Loans: Annual Report 1991–92,* London, DfEE

Department for Education and Employment (1993) *Career Development Loans: Annual Report 1992–93,* London, DfEE

Department for Education and Employment (1994) *Career Development Loans: Annual Report 1993-94,* London, DfEE.

Department for Education and Employment (1995) *Career Development Loans: Annual Report 1994-95*, London, DfEE

Department for Education and Employment (1996a) *Review of the Arrangements to Manage and Monitor the YT Guarantee,* London, DfEE

Department for Education and Employment (1996b) *Career Development Loans Reach Out to More Students*, Press release 218/96, 28.06.96, London, DfEE

Department for Education and Employment (1996c) *James Plaice Welcomes Help for Lifelong Learning*, Press release 418/96, 4.12.96, London, DfEE

Department for Education and Employment (1996d) *Over £250 Million Spent on Training with Career Development Loans*, Press release 119/96, 11.04.96, London, DfEE

Department for Education and Employment (1996e) *£27 Million Cash Aid for Students in Need.* Press release 263/96, 16.08.96, London, DfEE

Department for Education and Employment (1996f) *Career Development Loans: Annual Report 1995–96*, London, DfEE

Department for Education and Employment (1996g) *Statistics of Education, Student Support, England and Wales*, London, DfEE

Department for Education and Employment (1997) *Department for Education and Employment and Office for Standards in Education Departmental Report*, London, DfEE

Diamond, P (1996) The End of Discretionary Awards, *Education and the Law*, 8 (1) 61–68

Donnelly, C (1996a) *Studying on the Dole*, London, Unemployment Unit

Donnelly, C (1996b) *JSA and the 16-hour Rule: Opportunities or barriers?* Working Brief, London, Unemployment Unit and Youthaid, July, 18–19

Donnelly, C (1997) *The Chance of a Lifetime:How the benefit system creates barriers to lifetime learning for the unemployed*, London, Unemployment Unit

Eastwood, M and Casson, D (eds) (1992) *The Educational Grants Directory*, 1992 edition, London, Directory of Social Change

Employment Department (1995) Career development loans, *Labour Market Quarterly Report*, May, 10–12

Finn, D (1995) Studying while unemployed: the Jobseeker's Allowance and the 16-hour rule, *Adults Learning*, May, 272–274

Firth, D and Goffey, L (1996) *Individual Commitment: Tracking Learners' Decision Making*, London, HMSO

Fletcher-Campbell, F, Keys, W and Kendall, L (1994) *Discretionary Award Provision in England and Wales: A survey carried out by the National Foundation for Educational Research*, London, Calouste Gulbenkian Foundation

Full Employment UK (1995) *Labour and Learning Accounts: Report of employee consultations*, London, Full Employment UK

Further Education Funding Council (1994) *General Certificate of Education Advanced Level and Advanced Supplementary Qualifications: National Survey Report*, Coventry, FEFC

Further Education Funding Council (1996a) *Corporate Plan 1996–97 to 1998–99*, Coventry, FEFC

Further Education Funding Council (1996b) *Students Numbers at Colleges in the Further Education Sector and External Institutions in England in 1995–96*, Press release, 17 December, Coventry, FEFC

Further Education Funding Council (1996c) *How to Apply for Funding 1997–98*, Coventry, FEFC

Further Education Funding Council (1996d) *Student Numbers, Retention, Achievements and Destinations at Colleges in the Further Education Sector in England in 1994–95*. Press release, 24 September, Coventry, FEFC

Further Education Funding Council (1997) *Mapping Provision: The provision of and participation in Further Education by students with learning difficulties and/or disabilities*, London, The Stationery Office Bookshops, FEFC

Further Education Unit (1993) *Paying Their Way: The experiences of adult learners in vocational education and training in FE colleges*, London, FEU

Further Education Unit, University of London Institute of Education and the Nuffield Foundation (1994) *GNVQs 199–94: A National Survey Report*, London, FEU

Further Education Unit (1994a) *Tackling Targets*, London, FEU

Further Education Unit (1994b) Staying on or dropping out, *FEU Newsletter*, Spring, 8–9

Gallie, D and White, M (1993) *Employee Commitment and the Skills Revolution: First findings from the Employment in Britain Survey*, London, Policy Studies Institute

Garner, L and Imeson, R (1996) More bricks in the wall, *Journal of Access Studies*, 1996 Spring 11 (1) 97–110

Gray, J, Jesson, D and Tranmer, M (1993) *Boosting post-16 Participation in Full-time Education: A study of some key factors*, Youth Cohort Report No 20, London, Employment Department

Green, A and Ainley, P (1995) *Progression and the Targets in post-16 Education and Training*, Post-16 Education Centre Report, London, Institute of Education

Hauser, R (1992) 'The Decline in College Entry among African-Americans: Findings in search of an explanation', in P. Sniderman et al (eds) *Prejudice, Politics and Race in America Today*, Stanford, Stanford University Press, 271–306

Hauser, R and Anderson, D (1991) Post high school plans and aspiration of black and white high school seniors 1976–86, *Sociology of Education*, 64, 22–30

Hedoux, J (1981) Les non-publics de la formation collective, *Education Permanente*, 61, 89–105

Heller, D (1996) *Tuition Prices, Financial Aid, and Access to Public Higher Education: A state level analysis* Paper presented at the Annual Meeting of the American Educational Research Association, New York, April

Hinds, D (1997) Poor show: lack of dicretionary grants is threatening the future of British dance and drama training, *Times Educational Supplement,* 7 February

HMI (1991) *Student Completion Rates in Further Education Courses,* London (DES 281/91/ns)

HMI (1993) *Education for Adults in Further Education,* 405/92/NS, London, Department for Education and Employment

Hunt, J and Jackson, H (1992) *Vocational Education and the Adult Unwaged,* London, Kogan Page

Hyde, W (1992) Finance for adult learning: An overview of current provision, *Adults Learning,* 3 (9) 228–231

IFF (1994) *CDL Participants Survey,* London, IFF Research Ltd.

Jones, H (1994) The European Social Fund: A brief introduction to its structures and processes, *Adults Learning,* February, 145–146

Kennedy, H (1997) *Learning Works: Widening participation in further education,* Coventry, Further Education Council

Kensington and Chelsea College (1995) *Reports Arising from Surveys of Full-time and Part-time Students,* unpublished

Leslie, L and Brinkman, P (1987) Student price response in higher education: the student demand studies, *Journal of Higher Education* 58 (2) 181–204

Leslie, L and Brinkman, P (1988) *The Economic Value of Higher Education,* San Francisco, Jossey-Bass

Liberal Democrats (1996) *The Key to Lifelong Learning Proposals for Tertiary Education in England and Wales,* Policy Paper 18, London, Liberal Democrat Publications Ltd.

Lindley, R M (1991) 'Individuals, Human Resources and Markets', in J Stevens and R Mackay (eds) *Training and Competitiveness,* NEDO, Policy Issues Series, London, Kogan Page

Littlefield, D (1995) CBI: Who should pay for training part-timers? *People Management,* February, 19–20

McGivney, V (1990) *Education's for Other People: Access to education for non-participant adults. A Research Report,* Leicester, NIACE

McGivney, V (1992) *Motivating Unemployed Adults to Undertake Education and Training. Some British and other European findings,* Leicester, NIACE

McGivney, V (1994) *Wasted Potential: Training and Career Development for Part-time and Temporary Workers,* Leicester, NIACE

McGivney, V (1996) *Staying or Leaving the Course: Non-completion and retention of Mature Students in Further and Higher Education,* Leicester, NIACE

McHugh et al (1993) *Why Take NVQs? Perceptions of candidates in the South West.* Lancaster University, Centre for Study of Education and Training

McPherson, M (1978) 'The Demand for Higher Education', in D Brenemann and C Finn (eds) *Public Policy and Private Higher Education,* Washington, Brookings Institution

McPherson, M and Schapiro, M (1991) *Keeping College Affordable: Government and equal opportunity, Washington DC,* Brookings Institution

McQuail, S (1993) *No Childcare No Training: TECs, training providers and childcare allowances,* London, Daycare Trust/NCVO

Maguire, M, Hasluck, C and Green, A (1996) *Identifying Target Groups for Individual Commitment Policies,* London, Department for Education and Employment, Research Studies RS28

Maguire, M, Maguire, S and Felstead, A (1993) *Factors Influencing Individual Commitment to Lifetime Learning: A Literature Review,* Leicester, Centre for Labour Market Studies

Mansell, P (1997) When the bus stops, *FE NOW!* 15, 1997

Manson-Smith, D (ed) (1993) *Paying for Training,* Glasgow, The Planning Exchange

Martinez, P (1995a) *Student Retention in Further and Adult Education: The Evidence,* Mendip Paper 084, Bristol, FEDA

Martinez, P (1995b) Turning in and dropping out. *FE Now!* 21, 27

Maxwell, E (1994) Charities face more pressure to help, *Times Educational Supplement,* 14 October, 6

Meager, M. and Williams, M. (1994) *The Case for National Equality in Employment Targets: A Consultation Paper*, Falmer, Institute of Manpower Studies

Medway, J and Penney, R (1994) *Factors Affecting Successful Completion – The Isle of Wight College: A Case Study,* unpublished Paper, RP, 780, London, FEU

Mortenson, T (1990) *The Impact of Increased Loan Utilization among Low Family Income Students,* Iowa City, American College Testing Program

Mumper, M and Vander Ark (1991) Evaluating the Stafford Student Loan Programme: Current problems and prospects for reform, *Journal of Higher Education,* 62 (1) 62–78

Murray, I (1996) Career Development Loans: take-up continues to disappoint, *Working Brief* (62) 7–10

Nash, I (1994a) No way out of the money maze, *Times Educational Supplement,* 8 April, 11–12

National Association for Educational Guidance for Adults (1994) *Affording Adult Learning: Financial barriers to access and progression,* Glasgow, NAEGA

National Commission on Education (1995) *Learning to Succeed – The Way Ahead*, London, NCE

National Institute of Adult and Continuing Education (1994) *Learning Opportunities for Adults with Learning and/or Disabilities: Evidence for the FEFC Committee of Enquiry*, Leicester, NIACE

National Institute of Adult Education (1970) *Adequacy of Provision*, Leicester, NIAE

Orfield, G (1992) Money, equity and college access, *Harvard Educational Review,* 62, 337–372

Osborn, M, Withnall, A, and Charnley, A H(1980) Review of existing research in adult and continuing aducation, *The Disadvantaged*, Vol. 3, Leicester, NIACE

Page, C (1996) A problem shared, *FE NOW!* 27, 19

Payne, J (1991) *Women, Training and the Skills Shortage: The case for public investment*, London, Policy Studies Institute

Payne, J (1995) *Routes Beyond Compulsory Schooling*, Employment Department Research Series Youth Cohort Report No. 32, Sheffield, Employment Department

Payne, J and Callender, C (1997) *Student Loans: Who borrows and why?* London, Policy Studies Institute

Payne, J, Cheng, Y and Witherspoon, S (1996) *Education and Training for 16-18 year olds: Individual paths and national trends,* London, Policy Studies Institute

People and Work Unit (1990) *The Older Long-term Unemployed*, Newport, Gwent

Rawlinson, S (1996) *Further Education: An employer's factfile,* Falmer, The Institute for Employment Studies

Rigg, M (1989) *Training in Britain: A study of funding, activity, and attitudes* Training Agency, London, HMSO

Robertson, D (1995) 'The reform of higher education for social equity, individual choice and mobility,' in *Higher Education in a Learning Society*, School of Education, University of Durham, Durham, 46–66

Robertson, D (1996) 'Mutuality in the Learning Market – the Learning Bank as a durable solution to the funding crisis?', in F Coffield (ed) *Higher Education and Lifelong Learning*, Newcastle, Department of Education, University of Newcastle, 115–128

Robinson, P (1996) *Rhetoric and Reality:Britain's new vocational qualifications,* London, Centre for Economic Performance, LSE

Sargant, N (1991) *Learning and Leisure: A study of adult participation in learning and its policy implications,* Leicester, NIACE

Sharp, C (1996) *Review of Qualifications for 16–19 Year Olds: Completion of A Level and GNVQ courses: A Literature Review*, National Foundation for Educational Research

Smith, G and Bailey, V (1993) *Staying the Course*, London, BTEC

Somers, P and St John, E (1993) Assessing the impact of Financial Aid Offers on enrolment decisions, *Journal of Student Financial Aid,* 23 (3) 7–12

Spady, W G (1970) Dropouts from Higher Education: An interdisciplinary review and synthesis, *Interchange*, 1, 64–85

Spady, W G (1971) Dropouts from Higher Education: Toward an empirical model, *Interchange*, 2, 38–625

Spours, K (forthcoming) 'Student Retention and Successful Completion: Staff perceptions of issues affecting institutional capability', Section Six in *Management and Policy Issues in Incorporated Colleges*, Working Paper, Post-16 Education Centre, London, Institute of Education

St John, E (1990) Price response in enrolment decisions: An analysis of the High School and beyond Sophmore Cohort, *Research in Higher Education,* 31, 161–76

St John, E (1991) What really influences minority enrolment? An analysis of the high school class of 1982, *Research in Higher Education,* 32, 141–58

St John, E (1993) Untangling the Web: Using price-response measures in enrolment projections, *Journal of Higher Education,* 64 (6) 676–695

St John, E and Noell, J (1989) The effects of student financial aid on access to higher education: an analysis of progress with special consideration of minority enrolment, *Research in Higher Education,* 30, 568–81

St John, E and Starkey, J (1995) An alternative to net price: Assessing the influence of prices and subsidies on within-year persistence, *Journal of Higher Education,* 66 (2) 156–186

Stampen, J O and Cabrera, A F (1986) Explaining the effects of student aid on attrition, *Journal of Student Financial Aid,* 16, 28–40

Stampen, J O and Cabrera, A F (1988) The targeting and packaging of student aid and its effect on attrition, *Economics of Education Review,* 7, 15–27

Steedman, H and Green, A (1996) *Widening Participation in Further Education and Training: A Survey of the Issues. A Report to the Further Education Funding Council,* London, London School of Economics, Centre for Economic Performance

Tinto, V (1975) Dropout from Higher Education: A theoretical synthesis of recent research, *Review of Educational Research,* 45, 89–125

Tinto, V (1982) Limits of theory and practice in student attrition, *Journal of Higher Education,* 53, 687–700

Tinto, V (1987) *Leaving College: Rethinking the Causes and Cures of Student Attrition,* Chicago, University of Chicago Press

Tinto, V (1993) *Leaving College: Rethinking the Causes and Cures of Student Attrition* (2nd edition), Chicago, University of Chicago Press

Training Agency (1989) *Training in Britain: A Study of Funding, Activity and Attitudes. The Main Report,* Sheffield, Training Agency

Tremlett, N, Park, A and Dundon-Smith, D S (1995) *Individual Commitment to Learning: Further Findings from the Individual's Survey,* Employment Department Research Series No. 54, London, SCPR

Uden, T (1994) *Will to Learn. Individual Commitment and Adult Learning. A Policy Discussion Paper,* Leicester, NIACE

Unwin, L (1995) *Staying the Course: A Study of Full-time Students in South and East Cheshire,* unpublished report

Velez, W (1985) Finishing College: The effects of college type, *The Sociology of Education,* 58, 191–200

Wilson, A (1996) *Inland Revenue Statistics,* London, HMSO

Wirral Metropolitan College (1993) *Financial Barriers to Further and Higher Education for Adult Students,* Wirral Metropolitan College

Woodley, A (1994) *Explaining Non-completion Rates in Scottish Universities,* British Staff College, Mendip Paper 060

Youthaid NATFHE (1993) *Credit Limit: Critical Assessment of the Training Credit Pilot Scheme,* London, NATFHE

ADDITIONAL REFERENCES

House of Commons Hansard Written Answers, Column 262, 13 February 1997

House of Commons Hansard Written Answers, Column 340, 30 January 1997

House of Commons Hansard Written Answers, Column 267, 29 January 1997

House of Commons Hansard Written Answers, Column 265, 29 January 1997

DfEE fax 20 February 1997, ESF Objectives 3, Further Education Sector Allocations